C000255544

TEA

A MISCELLANY STEEPED WITH TRIVIA, HISTORY AND RECIPES

EMILY KEARNS

summersdale

TEA

Summersdale Publishers Ltd
46 West Street
Chichester
West Sussex
PO19 1RP
UK

www.summersdale.com

Printed and bound in the Czech Republic

ISBN: 978-1-84953-679-0

Substantial discounts on bulk quantities of Summersdale books are available to corporations, professional associations and other organisations. For details contact Nicky Douglas by telephone: +44 (0) 1243 756902, fax: +44 (0) 1243 786300 or email: nicky@summersdale.com.

FOR ANDREW AND PHOEBE

CONTENTS

COME ALONG INSIDE... WE'LL SEE IF TEA AND BUNS CAN MAKE THE WORLD A BETTER PLACE.

Kenneth Grahame, *The Wind in the Willows*

INTRODUCTION

From its accidental discovery in China several thousands of years ago to its evolution into the global beverage of choice and one of the biggest industries in the world, it's fair to say that tea has achieved rather a lot. Tea is a way of life for so many of us. Whether used in ceremony or through habit, whether via leaves or the humble teabag, how many of us find the day hasn't started until we're at least one tea down?

This book looks at the history of the wonder brew, from how it was discovered to how word of it spread across the globe and made its way to Europe, and how the industry has grown to offer a huge variety of teas. It also covers the health benefits of drinking tea, as well as the different rituals practised around the world, not to mention the sticklers for tea perfection who continue to debate the ultimate serve.

So kick off your shoes, put the kettle on, and let's raise a toast to tea and all those who make it.

CHAPTER 1
TEA 101

For me, starting the day without a pot of tea would be a day forever out of kilter.

Bill Drummond

WHAT IS TEA?

The tea we generally consume consists of the dried leaves of the *Camellia sinensis*, commonly referred to as the tea plant. The plant can be found growing as an evergreen bush or tree, and produces small white flowers and bitter-tasting fruit among its sharp, thick and shiny leaves. The two main subspecies of tea plant are *Camellia sinensis sinensis*, the original Chinese variety, and *Camellia sinensis assamica*, which is native to India and is what you probably know as Assam. The first teas to go to market were of the green variety, and it was only through experimenting with the manufacturing process, by drying the leaves for longer, that tea producers came up with black tea.

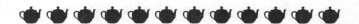

*Teas vary as much in appearance
as the different faces of men.*

Emperor Huizong of Song

THE REAL THING

Any kind of 'tea' which is not derived
from the *Camellia sinensis* – i.e.
peppermint, chamomile, rooibos,
etc. – is not strictly tea. However,
with many a tea drinker turning
to herbal varieties and the health
benefits seemingly plentiful, I have
adopted a more liberal meaning
and included some other 'teas'
in this book (see A–Z of Tea).

WHERE DOES IT GROW?

The tea we know and love originated in China and was later introduced to India by the British. These days tea is mass-produced in some 30 countries across the globe, but the four biggest producers, in order, are China, India, Kenya and Sri Lanka. Of the best-known varieties, China produces green, white, black and oolong tea; India produces Assam and Darjeeling; Kenya produces black, green, yellow and white teas; and Sri Lanka produces Ceylon.

I am a hardened and shameless tea drinker, who for twenty years diluted his meals with only the infusion of the plant; who with tea amused the evening, with tea solaced the midnight and with tea welcomed the morning.

Samuel Johnson

HOW IS IT HARVESTED?

Tea plants are grown from seed or cuttings and can take up to three years before they are harvest-ready. It generally takes between four and 12 years for a tea plant to bear seed, so propagation from cutting is generally preferred. Plants are kept short for ease of harvesting, despite their ability to reach around 15 m in height. Pruned plants will also produce more new shoots, which means tender and better-quality leaves as well as, ultimately, a better-quality brew. Tea is harvested in seasons, referred to as 'flushes', from which derive descriptive terms such as 'first-flush Darjeeling', for example. Tea leaves are generally 'plucked' by hand, using a specific action, as this method delivers a higher-quality product. However, machine harvesting also takes place in areas where there aren't the hands available to get the job done, or where the tea leaves are destined for blends (see The Hows and Wheres of Tea for more on tea-making processes).

WHAT HAPPENS NEXT?

Since the 1930s, the most widely employed method of production for black tea intended for use in teabags has been 'crush, tear and curl' or CTC. This stage takes place after the raw leaves have been left to wither, in order to reduce their water content, and involves a set of cylindrical serrated rollers through which the tea leaves are passed and, well, crushed, torn and curled. Leaves intended for other teas, such as green, tend to be hand-harvested to preserve quality and then rolled. After this stage, the leaves will be left to rest and oxidise for however long their intended tea style requires, before being dried in an oven.

WHO DRINKS IT?

Who doesn't drink it? In the UK alone some 165 million cups of tea are consumed every day, and globally it is the second most-consumed liquid after water. That daily total equates to 60.2 billion cups a year, a quite startling figure. Perhaps surprisingly, the largest tea-drinking nation per capita is Turkey, with Ireland and the UK coming second and third respectively.

TEA CONSUMPTION PER CAPITA

China is the largest consumer of tea, with 1.6 billion lb of it consumed a year, but a look at per-capita consumption globally paints a different picture:

(1) Turkey: 6.96 lb (3.16 kg)

(2) Ireland: 4.83 lb (2.2 kg)

(3) UK: 4.28 lb (1.94 kg)

(4) Russia: 3.05 lb (1.38 kg)

(5) Morocco: 2.68 lb (1.22 kg)

(6) New Zealand: 2.63 lb (1.19 kg)

(7) Egypt: 2.23 lb (1.01 kg)

(8) Poland: 2.2 lb (1 kg)

(9) Japan: 2.13 lb (0.97 kg)

(10) Saudi Arabia: 1.98 lb (0.90 kg)

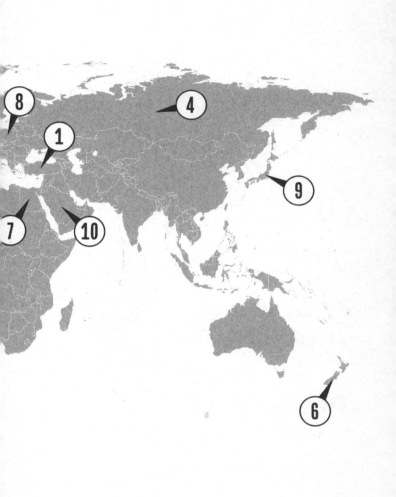

NOW LET'S SEE WHO DRINKS THE LEAST TEA PER CAPITA:

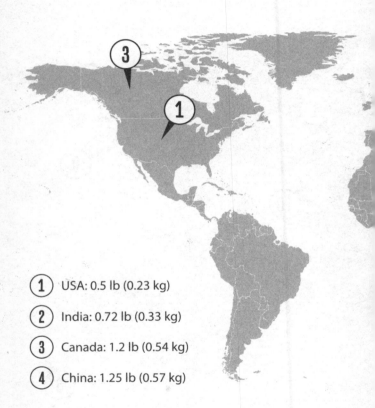

1. USA: 0.5 lb (0.23 kg)
2. India: 0.72 lb (0.33 kg)
3. Canada: 1.2 lb (0.54 kg)
4. China: 1.25 lb (0.57 kg)

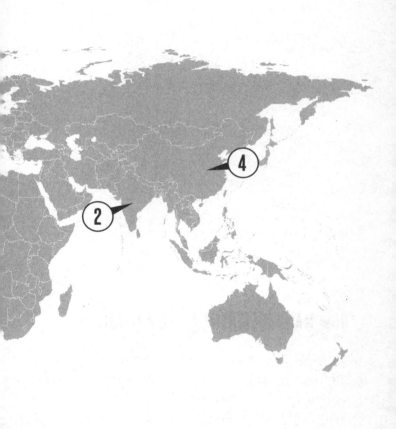

(Source: Euromonitor)

THE PERFECT SERVE?

96 per cent of the tea drunk
in Britain is brewed via a
teabag and 98 per cent of us
prefer milk in our brew.

HOW MANY DIFFERENT TYPES ARE THERE?

According to the UK Tea & Infusions Association
(formerly the UK Tea Council), there are around 1,500
varieties of tea. However, these all stem from six
main types: black, green, oolong, white, yellow and
fermented tea.

I SAY LET THE
WORLD GO TO HELL,

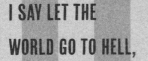

BUT I SHOULD ALWAYS
HAVE MY TEA.

Fyodor Dostoevsky,
Notes from Underground

CHAPTER 2
TEA: A TIMELINE

Tea tempers the spirit and harmonises the mind, dispels lassitude and relieves fatigue, awakens thought and prevents drowsiness.

Lu Yu, *The Classic of Tea*

BC 2737 – According to legend, green tea is discovered by Chinese Emperor Shennong when some stray dry tea bush leaves fall into a pot of boiling water. Upon drinking the resulting liquid the emperor claims its properties 'give joy to the body and sparkle to the eyes'.

*c.*332 **AD** – Tea has by now come to be regarded as China's national drink.

Sixth century – Trade in tea starts between China and its neighbouring countries, with sacks of the sought-after leaves exchanged for horses.

*c.*780 – Lu Yu, widely recognised as the daddy of Chinese tea, writes a book dedicated to the beverage, *Cha Jing* (*The Classic of Tea*), focusing on the plant's cultivation and preparation. It is soon considered essential reading for all Chinese tea farmers, merchants and drinkers.

Ninth century – Tea is introduced to Japan by Buddhist monks who bring it back from their pilgrimage to China. The Japanese go positively wild for the infusion and many will eventually build a way of life around it, but for many years it remains an expensive habit enjoyed only by the rich and privileged.

1368–1644 – During the Ming Dynasty, Chinese producers devise a method of manufacturing tea leaves that will ensure they last longer and travel better. The tea leaves are naturally oxidised for longer to create a darker dried end product. Black tea is born.

1420s – The Japanese tea ceremony is introduced by Zen priest Murata Jukō, elevating tea drinking to something of an art-form-cum-religion.

1599 – Queen Elizabeth I founds the East India Company in order to forge trade links with Asia. It will go on to hold a monopoly over the tea industry in the British colonies until the mid-nineteenth century.

As well as trading in tea, the East India Company, often informally known as 'John Company', traded in many other commodities, including cotton, silk, indigo dye, salt, saltpetre and opium. The company, which had its own private armies to control the territories it operated in, also had its own coat of arms and flag.

1610 – The first shipment of tea arrives in Europe, in Amsterdam, aboard a Dutch trading vessel. The Dutch market the tea as a medicinal beverage, but prices are so high that only the aristocracy can afford it.

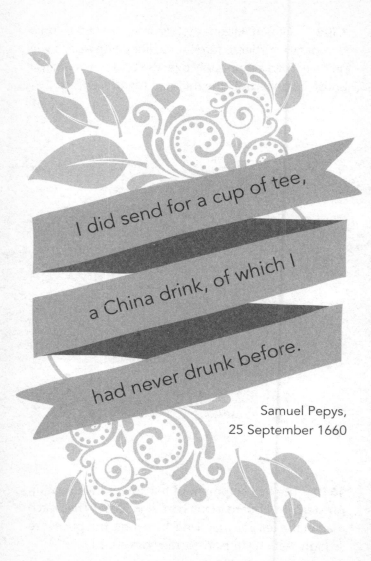

I did send for a cup of tee, a China drink, of which I had never drunk before.

Samuel Pepys,
25 September 1660

1650s – The first shipment of tea arrives in London, making its way from Holland. Soon afterwards, tea drinking is taken up by Catherine of Braganza, wife of King Charles II, and the practice spreads like wildfire through the upper echelons of society. In fact, tea is so on-trend that consumption of alcohol declines.

1669 – After convincing the British government to enforce a ban on Dutch imports of tea, the East India Company takes control of the market.

1700s – Thanks to improved trade links, Chinese tea begins to arrive in Egypt, Iran, Russia and Turkey.

1700s – The Russians invent the samovar, which soon becomes integral to Russian tea-drinking culture. The receptacle is used to brew a highly concentrated liquid, allowing drinkers to add varying amounts of water as their taste buds require. Tea drinkers, it would appear, have always been quite particular.

1706 – Thomas Twining opens the first tearoom in Britain, in what used to be a coffee house, at 216 Strand, London. With its teas a mainstay on British supermarket shelves for centuries, Twinings' original tearoom still sits happily on the Strand and operates as a museum and tea shop.

TEA TOLERANCE

In 1706 the book *Wholesome Advice Against the Abuse of Hot Liquors* is published in Britain, warning against excessive consumption of tea, coffee and hot chocolate, claiming the steaming liquid causes one's insides to heat up quickly and that 'excess of heat is the most common cause of sickness and death'. In 1748, John Wesley, founding father of the Methodists, claims that all should abstain from the hearty brew as it causes one to harbour a nervous disposition, among other health issues. He is deemed to be very convincing in his arguments and even counsels abstainers on how to politely refuse a cup of tea. We didn't pay that much attention, though, did we?

TEA'S PROPER USE IS TO
AMUSE THE IDLE,
AND RELAX THE STUDIOUS,

AND DILUTE THE FULL
MEALS OF THOSE WHO
CANNOT USE EXERCISE,
AND WILL NOT USE
ABSTINENCE.

Samuel Johnson, 1757

1767 – Britain passes a series of acts imposing taxes on tea and many other goods imported into the British–American colonies. Following the news, many Americans boycott British imports, leading to a rise in the smuggling of tea into America from Holland.

SMUGGLING

In eighteenth-century Britain tea was no longer considered a beverage for the elite; now everybody wanted a fix, but the heavy taxes meant few could afford it. Smugglers stepped in to provide Britons with the brew they craved. At the height of the trade, as much as 7 million lb of illegal tea was imported into the country annually, compared with the legal import of 5 million lb.

1773 – The cargo of three tea ships is thrown into Boston harbour by the American Sons of Liberty in a political protest against escalating taxes levied on tea by the East India Company. The act of rebellion becomes known as the Boston Tea Party and in 1774 further 'tea parties' are reported along the east coast of America, in Maine, New York, Philadelphia, Maryland and North Carolina. The taxation protests continue and the debacle effectively kick-starts the American Revolution.

Last Night 3 Cargoes of Bohea Tea were emptied into the Sea. This Morning a Man of War sails.

This is the most magnificent Movement of all. There is a Dignity, a Majesty, a Sublimity, in this last Effort of the Patriots, that I greatly admire... This Destruction of the Tea is so bold, so daring, so firm, intrepid and inflexible, and it must have so important Consequences, and so lasting, that I cant but consider it as an Epocha in History.

Diary of John Adams,
17 December 1773

So inscrutable is the arrangement of causes and consequences in this world, that a two-penny duty on tea, unjustly imposed in a sequestered part of it, changes the condition of all its inhabitants.

Thomas Jefferson

AMERICANS OPT FOR COFFEE

After the events of the Boston Tea Party
many Americans switch hot beverage
allegiances and start drinking coffee instead.
In 1774 the town of Dedham, Massachusetts
outlaws the consumption of tea, appoints
a committee to police the ban and calls
for any resident caught drinking it to have
their name dragged through the dirt.

Coffee is not my cup of tea.

Samuel Goldwyn

1809 – Jane Austen is placed in charge of the key to the tea chest at Chawton, the Austens' cottage in Hampshire, where she spent the last eight years of her life. Tea is so expensive it is kept under lock and key to prevent pilfering.

I am sorry to hear that there has been a rise in tea. I do not mean to pay Twining till later in the day, when we may order a fresh supply.

Jane Austen writing to her sister Cassandra, 6 March 1814

1820s – A blend of tea flavoured with bergamot oil begins to become popular in England. The citrus notes of this blend were intended to reproduce the flavour of the finest Chinese black teas, and in fact even became the subject of a court case in 1837, when Brocksop & Co. were found to have supplied tea 'artificially scented, and, drugged with bergamot in this country'. However, despite these bumpy beginnings, the blend becomes known as Earl Grey and remains popular to this day.

THE REAL EARL GREY

Charles Grey, the 2nd Earl Grey, was Prime Minister of the United Kingdom from 1830 to 1834. He was deeply involved in the Reform Act of 1832 and the Slavery Abolition Act of 1832, but the true explanation for his connection to the famous tea that bears his name is hotly debated. One romantic story is that the tea was given to him by a Chinese mandarin in gratitude after Grey had saved his son from death by drowning, though this is widely believed to be apocryphal. A more pragmatic alternative theory comes from the Grey family themselves, who explain that the blend was developed by a Chinese mandarin to suit the water at the family seat, Howick Hall in Northumberland, with its heavy preponderance of lime. Whichever story is true, the fact remains that Earl Grey is a distinctive and unforgettable tea blend, with millions of devotees around the world.

1845 – This year sees the launch of what is considered to be the first true tea clipper. The brainchild of American naval architect John W. Griffiths, *Rainbow* makes the journey from New York to Canton in 102 days, shaving two weeks off the previous record for that journey.

1848 – Scottish botanist Robert Fortune is employed by the Horticultural Society to set sail on a plant-hunting expedition to bring tea plants from China back to Britain.

1859 – Britons introduce large-scale tea growing to India, with the first crop taking root in Darjeeling.

1860s – Tea is introduced to Sri Lanka by the British after the country's myriad coffee plantations fall foul of an agricultural parasite and are wiped out. Briton James Taylor sets up a tea plantation in Kandy, a factory follows a few years later and, in 1873, Sri Lanka's first tea shipment arrives in London.

A HEALTHY OPTION

Before the twentieth century, boiled beverages were considered safer to drink, so many opted for tea over water.

1866 – Tea clippers laden with cargo take to racing each other back to port, the public keenly following their progress via the press. This year sees a heated 'sprint' from China back to London – a passage of more than 14,000 miles – involving the clippers *Ariel*, *Fiery Cross*, *Serica*, *Taeping* and *Taitsing*, which becomes known as the Great Tea Race. After more than three months at sea, *Taeping* and *Ariel* are neck and neck with the former docking just 28 minutes before the latter.

1903 – The Trans-Siberian Railway opens this year, allowing the rapid transport of goods, including tea, from China to Moscow, Berlin and Paris.

THE TEA FIELDS OF CEYLON ARE AS TRUE A MONUMENT
TO COURAGE AS IS THE LION AT WATERLOO.

Arthur Conan Doyle

1904 – New York tea and coffee merchant Thomas Sullivan invents the beloved teabag – by accident. Sullivan bags up samples of loose tea, intending for the contents to be removed before consumption. But customers find it not only brews better in the porous fabric bag but also greatly simplifies the process. Raise those teacups high in a toast to Thomas Sullivan.

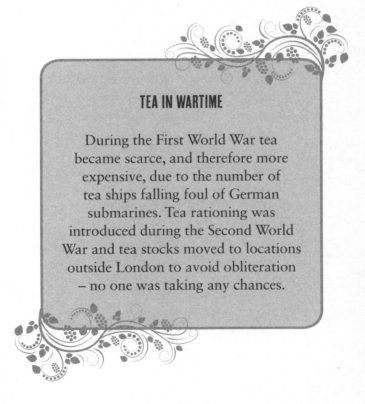

TEA IN WARTIME

During the First World War tea became scarce, and therefore more expensive, due to the number of tea ships falling foul of German submarines. Tea rationing was introduced during the Second World War and tea stocks moved to locations outside London to avoid obliteration – no one was taking any chances.

1915

Supplies for the army
*In its large warehouse in Cutler-street,
EC, the Port of London Authority
is quietly playing a useful part in
assuring the comfort of his Majesty's
Forces. From the enormous stocks
of tea, totalling at the present time
about 18,500,000 lb, which are under
Customs' control at these bonded
warehouses, large supplies are being
regularly despatched, to meet the
requirements of the Government.
Quite recently, for example, the Port
Authority's staff at Cutler-street
was called upon to blend and pack
no less than 57,000 lb of tea in
connection with the execution of a
single demand of the War Office.*

...

Altogether the Cutler-street warehouses can store 20,000,000 lb of tea, which is equivalent to something like one-fourth of the stock in all the bonded warehouses of the United Kingdom at a recent date. The bulk of it comes from India and Ceylon, with Java qualities more in evidence than usual, owing to the difficulties in the way of re-exportation from Holland, and China growths still show a steadily diminishing proportion.

The Daily Telegraph, 16 July 1915

1930 – The CTC (crush, tear, curl) method is introduced to tea picking, which paves the way for tea production on a grand scale. And this is a big year for tea, as it also sees the invention of the heat-sealed paper teabag by Bostonian William Hermanson. The paper teabags started as little sacks and evolved into the square variety in 1944.

'IT'S THE TASTE'

When PG Tips tea is first introduced to Britain in the 1930s, it is marketed as a pre-dinner digestive aid called 'Pre-Gest-Tee'. After the Second World War, however, new labelling regulations disallow the insinuation that tea aids digestion and thus it becomes known as PG Tips. The 'Tips' half of the name refers to the use of only the top two layers, or 'tips', of the tea plant in production.

Is there no Latin word for Tea? Upon my soul, if I had known that I would have let the vulgar stuff alone.

Hilaire Belloc, *On Nothing & Kindred Subjects*

WOULDN'T IT BE DREADFUL TO LIVE IN A COUNTRY

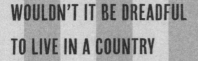

WHERE THEY DIDN'T HAVE TEA?

Noël Coward

1997 – The Ethical Tea Partnership is formed. Originally called the Tea Sourcing Partnership, this not-for-profit organisation's aim is to improve working conditions within the industry and promote the sustainability of tea production, all while keeping a watchful eye on its impact on the environment. The ETP currently works with producers to run sustainability programmes in Argentina, Brazil, Burundi, China, India, Indonesia, Kenya, Malawi, Mozambique, Papua New Guinea, Rwanda, South Africa, Sri Lanka, Tanzania and Uganda.

2014 – Tea lovers continue to hanker after the perfect serve, but it seems the ultimate cup of tea comes with a hefty price tag (£7,700 to be precise). Beverage innovation company Bkon launches the Craft Brewer, which offers a new and allegedly improved tea-infusing method using 'RAIN' (reverse atmospheric infusion) technology. Loose leaves and water are placed in the brewing chamber of the Craft Brewer machine, the air is drawn out to create a vacuum, and the negative pressure brings the tea leaves to the surface, which, according to Bkon, draws out a fuller flavour than your average teapot.

Tea is one of the mainstays of civilisation in this country.

Samuel Pepys,
25 September 1660

CHAPTER 3
THE HOWS AND WHERES OF TEA

The first cup moistens my lips and throat...
The fifth lifts me to the realms
of the unwinking gods.

Chinese Mystic, Tang Dynasty

As we've already learnt, legend has it that tea was first discovered in China 5,000 years ago. The British then introduced the commercial production of tea to India and now some 30 countries produce it on a grand scale. Let's get to grips with what comes from where and how the magic happens.

TEA PRODUCTION: THE STAGES

All teas are produced using a variation on the stages below: some might skip a stage, while others see the duration of each stage shortened or lengthened depending on the desired result.

- **Picking** – Tea leaf 'plucking' is considered something of an art and is a labour-intensive process. The tea shoot should be grasped between thumb and forefinger and pulled from the plant with a sharp movement of the arm and shoulder. Most high-quality teas are still plucked by hand, while commercial production for use in teabags generally uses heavy-duty machinery. Around 5 lb of fresh tea leaves will equate to 1 lb of the finished product.

- **Withering** – Tea leaves are spread thinly over large trays to semi-dry, losing some of their moisture. The length of time spent withering depends on the type of tea; some producers will use fans to help the process along.

- **Rolling/crushing** – The leaves are then rolled, or crushed, to allow the release of the natural enzymes, which will help with the next process – oxidisation. The rolling method falls into two categories: 'orthodox' and CTC (crush, tear, curl). The orthodox machine rolls the leaf, while the CTC method sees the tea leaves shredded in a cylindrical machine with serrated blades. The CTC method tends to be reserved for teas to be used in blends, while the higher-quality variants will be prepared via the orthodox machine.

- **Oxidising** – The next stage sees the leaves once again spread out on large trays for several hours in a climate-controlled room. Again, the time spent oxidising depends on the variety of tea. For example, this stage would be lengthier for leaves destined for black teas.

- **Firing** – The leaves are then exposed to high temperatures to prevent any further oxidisation and to lock in flavour, before being sorted into leaf sizes – the smaller pieces generally ending up in teabags and the larger being sold as loose-leaf teas.

FULL FLUSH

Each tea season, or 'flush', has its own unique characteristics. The number of flushes in each tea-producing country depends on the suitability of the seasons for cultivation, but typically the flushes occur twice a year in spring and summer. In India there are four flushes – first, second, monsoon and autumnal – each considered to produce a different crop.

A woman is like a tea bag – you never know how strong she is until she gets in hot water.

Eleanor Roosevelt

ARGENTINA

Annual production:
100,000 tons

Main tea-growing regions:
Misiones and Corrientes provinces

Teas of note:
Black tea, primarily used in blends

- Argentina has been producing tea since the 1950s, the majority of its crop winding up in American iced teas.

- The nation may be one of the biggest producers of black tea, but its native yerba mate herbal tea is the more well-known (see A–Z of Tea).

BANGLADESH

Annual production:
61,500 tons

Main tea-growing regions:
Sylhet

Teas of note:
Black, green, white

- Tea production began in Bangladesh in 1857 and today the country boasts 162 tea estates in the district of Sylhet.
- The teas are known for their strong and spicy character and in recent years organic farming methods have been introduced in many of the estates.

BURMA

Annual production:
32,000 tons

Main tea-growing regions:
Tawngpeng

Teas of note:
Green, fermented tea (lahpet)

- The main tea-growing region is located in the Shan state of eastern Burma, close to China's Yunnan province and sharing similar terrain.

- Burma's teas are generally produced for domestic consumption and are not widely available in the West.

- Burma is unusual in this list in that it cultivates several different teas designed to be eaten.

BURMA'S EDIBLE TEA

The country's most popular tea is lahpet, which is eaten as well as being served as a beverage. The tea leaves are pickled and generally prepared with sesame oil, and side orders of peas, peanuts, dried shrimp, garlic, coconut and ginger. The pickled tea leaves are considered something of a delicacy and are rolled out on special occasions.

Of all the fruit, the mango's the best; of all the meat, the pork's the best; and of all the leaves, lahpet's the best.

Burmese proverb

CHINA

Annual production:
1.7 million tons

Main tea-growing regions:
Anhui, Fujian, Guangdong, Guangxi, Guizhou, Hainan, Henan, Hubei, Hunan, Jiangsu, Jiangxi, Shaanxi, Shandong, Sichuan, Yunnan and Zhejiang provinces

Teas of note:
Black (Lapsang Souchong, Yunnan, Keemun), green (sencha, gunpowder), oolong (quilan), pu-erh, white (silver needle, pai mu tan), yellow (Huangshan Maofeng)

- China produces more tea than any other country in the world.
- Yunnan province in the far south-west is widely considered to be the most ancient of tea-growing regions and the birthplace of tea, claiming to have wild tea trees that are thousands of years old.

- China produces thousands of different types and grades of tea leaves – seriously mind-bending amounts.
- Leaf buds picked in the spring from mountainous tea-cultivating areas are considered to produce the best-quality teas.
- What we call 'black tea' the Chinese refer to as 'red tea', reserving the term 'black tea' for fermented teas.

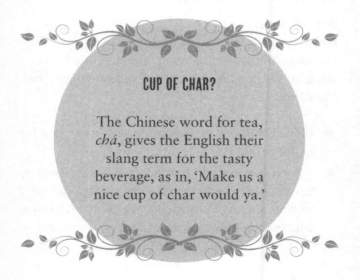

CUP OF CHAR?

The Chinese word for tea, *chá*, gives the English their slang term for the tasty beverage, as in, 'Make us a nice cup of char would ya.'

INDIA

Annual production:
1 million tons

Main tea-growing regions:
Assam, Darjeeling, Nilgiri

Teas of note:
Black (Assam, Darjeeling, Nilgiri, Sikkim), green (Assam green), white (Assam white)

- India comes second only to China in its annual production of tea.

- The Assam tea plant, or *Camellia sinensis assamica*, was first encountered in India by a British explorer in the early 1800s, being consumed on a very local level in drinks made from wild plants. However, commercial production didn't begin until 1834.

- Assam is the largest tea-growing area in the world and accounts for 55 per cent of India's annual tea production.

- Despite their teas being quite different in taste, the regions of Assam and Darjeeling lie only 120 miles apart.

- Nilgiri is an intensely aromatic tea, which is grown in southern India in the Western Ghats mountains, while Sikkim, which borders both Nepal and Tibet, produces rare teas with characteristics similar to Darjeeling.

TEA TASTING

Detecting the many subtle flavour variations of the world's teas is just as refined an art as wine or whisky tasting, and becoming a professional tea-taster requires an intensive five-year training period.

Chris Banks spent his career as a tea buyer for Lipton, and in the following passage, he describes his induction into the tea trade in the 1950s:

> *Prior to sailing off into the sunset, I had to undergo a crash course in tea tasting in a tall building at the top end of Shoreditch High Street where Lipton had their tea tasting, buying, packing and blending operation.*
>
> *The top floor accommodated a small army of experienced tasters and senior buyers, some of whom had experienced the world*

of tea 'out East'. A team of cheery girls took care of the seemingly endless washing up of tasting bowls and pots.

Endless trays of carefully brewed tea, which had been poured into white, uniformly sized bowls from miniature pots were laid in front of me along two massive wooden benches which also served to store hundreds of small sample tins. The tea came in sample form from individual estates via several tea brokers from all over the world, ranging from Darjeeling, Assam, Dooars, the Nilgiri Hills in South India, Ceylon, Java, Sumatra, Vietnam, Kenya – the list went on and on. Almost 1,600 teas representing anything up to 60,000 chests were tasted daily by a team of five or so tasters and blenders.

One of the main purposes of tasting was to ensure that there was no taint or foreign flavour which may have been picked up during the manufacture at the estate factory. This is vitally important, as one bad lot in a selection of 20 to 30 different teas from various origins would ruin an entire blend.

The buyer evaluates each tea invoice which represents a 'batch' of tea manufactured at the same time and under the same ambient conditions: this may be any quantity up to 80 chests depending on the capacity of the *individual estate. Based on the quality of flavour, leaf appearance and colour of the brew, as well as the infusion, the buyer will value accordingly.*

The more I tasted, the more fascinated I became. The tea industry covered an immense range of activities such as cultivation, manufacture, warehousing, tasting, buying, blending, marketing, packing and shipping all of which I was destined to experience first-hand. **"**

ANYONE WHO HAS USED THAT
COMFORTING PHRASE 'A NICE CUP OF TEA'
INVARIABLY MEANS INDIAN TEA.

George Orwell

TEA GROWING IN BLIGHTY

Yep, you did read that right. Cornish tea estate Tregothnan claims to 'put the English in English tea' and has been growing *Camellia sinensis* bushes since 2000. Deeming the weather in their corner of Cornwall (near Truro) to be temperate enough for tea cultivation, Tregothnan has enjoyed commercial acclaim with its range of teas, which are topped up with imported Assam to ensure the flavours are just right. The estate's most recent triumph, in 2014, saw Waitrose stocking its Classic Tea and Earl Grey varieties. Aside from Waitrose's favoured stocks, Tregothnan also produces teas including afternoon, Great British and green, as well as myriad herbal infusions, such as chamomile, echinacea, eucalyptus, manuka, red berry and peppermint, among others.

INDONESIA

Annual production:
150,100 tons

Main tea-growing regions:
Java

Teas of note:
Black (Java malabar), oolong (Sumatra oolong)

- The Dutch East India Company kick-started tea production in Indonesia in the early 1700s, choosing to sow the first seeds on the island of Sumatra. Most of Indonesia's tea is now grown on volcanic soil in the mountainous regions of the island of Java.

- The original seeds sown were from Chinese tea plants, but these did not take to the soil and so were replaced with Assam bushes from India.

- In the early 1900s Indonesian teas were popular throughout Britain and Europe, but the nation's industry suffered during the Second World War, as tea estates were abandoned, and did not recover for several decades.

IRAN

Annual production:
158,000 tons

Main tea-growing regions:
Gilan and Mazandaran provinces

Teas of note:
Black

- Iran began producing tea in the early 1900s and is now in the top 20 tea-producing countries in the world.
- Iranian teas are known for being smooth and light.

JAPAN

Annual production:
85,900 tons

Main tea-growing regions:
Kyoto, Kyushu, Mie, Nara
and Shizuoka prefectures

Teas of note:
Green (gyokuro, matcha, sencha), black

- Japanese tea growing tends to take place close to rivers, lakes and streams, in hilly areas of the country, where the mist and damp in the growing season strikes a balance with the warm climate.
- Although Japan produces some black teas, green tea is king here, both in terms of exports and in-country consumption.

KENYA

Annual production:
369,400 tons

Main tea-growing regions:
Cherangani Hills, Kericho
Highlands, Kissi Highlands,
Nandi

Teas of note:
Black (usually used in blends), green, white (nandi
safari, silver needle)

- Kenya is the third-largest tea-growing nation in the world and has been a serious contender in the industry since the early 1900s.

- Tea is generally cultivated in mountainous regions at altitudes of between 5,000 and 6,500 feet.

- While Kenya has always grown black teas, in more recent years growers have been experimenting in the production of green and white teas.

- Due to its position on the equator, Kenya is hot pretty much all year round and therefore the tea season never ends.

- As well as large growers producing tea on a massive scale, there is an abundance of smaller, independent growers creating high-quality small-batch teas.

MALAWI

Annual production:
53,500 tons

Main tea-growing regions:
Mulanje, Nkhata Bay, Thyolo

Teas of note:
Black

- Tea comes second only to cotton in Malawi in terms of commercial crops, with most being grown by artisan producers.
- In 1996 an EU-funded scheme to improve tea production saw the replanting of more than 1,800 hectares of tea plants, which has led to higher yields and a better-quality end product.

MOZAMBIQUE

Annual production:
22,000 tons

Main tea-growing regions:
Zambezi

Teas of note:
Black (generally used in
blends)

- Mozambique still produces a substantial crop each year, although production has waned in recent decades due to political unrest.
- The crops grown here make strong, black teas, which are mainly used in blends and end up in teabags.

THE FAIRTRADE FOUNDATION

The Fairtrade Foundation is a big supporter of the tea industry, working with farmers and labourers involved in all elements of the production process to protect the rights of employees, ensure comfortable working conditions and implement the fairest trade possible between growers and the rest of the supply chain. Profits earned from Fairtrade tea are pumped back into the communities from where it came, and invested in education, housing and healthcare. Fairtrade is committed to introducing a living wage for tea workers and is involved in a global project – Tea 2030 – to help build and maintain a sustainable tea industry for the future.

Coffee is a mere beverage; Tea is a way of life.

Miriam Novalle

NEPAL

Annual production:
18,730 tons

Main tea-growing regions:
Dhankuta, Ilam, Jhapa, Panchthar, Terhathum

Teas of note:
Black (Dhankuta, Ilam, Panchthar, Ruby Black),
green, oolong

- Nepalese tea gardens are generally located at high altitudes on steep mountainsides, similar to the terrain of Darjeeling in India.

- Black Nepalese teas are often likened to Darjeeling in terms of aroma and taste, and with some of the tea gardens located only 40 or 50 miles away from the famous Indian tea region it's not hard to see why.

- Nepal's tea industry was slower to grow than its neighbour India's, due to Nepal's independence from the British Empire which distanced it from economic development in the nineteenth century, as well as internal political turmoil. However, from the 1950s onwards, the tea industry was actively developed, undergoing privatisation, and playing a significant role in the eradication of rural poverty.

MAKING THE GRADE

Tea is often classified into grades to communicate to the drinker more about its quality. Tea grading is not a particularly simple process, with several different systems in place, but it all boils down (no pun intended) to how the tea has been handled post-harvest. The most widely used grading system sees tea classified as 'orthodox' or 'unorthodox' (CTC-produced teas) and tends to be used to grade black teas. The grade of tea can often reflect its caffeine content and tells the drinker how they should best brew the tea for the perfect serve.

RWANDA

Annual production:
22,500 tons

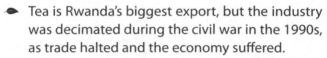

Main tea-growing regions:
Byumba, Cyangugu, Gikongoro, Gisenyi and Kibuye

Teas of note:
Black, green

- Tea is Rwanda's biggest export, but the industry was decimated during the civil war in the 1990s, as trade halted and the economy suffered.
- Heavy investment in the industry in more recent years has seen production go from strength to strength and the quality of the tea rise considerably.
- The most popular black teas are likened to Assam in flavour, although they are somewhat milder.
- Rwanda's tea crop provides vital income for over 30,000 smallholders and 60,000 households across the country. These smallholders produce more than 65 per cent of Rwanda's tea.

THE TEA PLANTATION OF THE DEEP SOUTH

Despite many attempts to cultivate tea in the USA during the nineteenth century, there is only one plantation in existence in America today – the Charleston Tea Plantation, on Wadmalaw Island, 20 miles south of Charleston, South Carolina. This is the birthplace of US brand American Classic Tea – 'beverage of South Carolina', so we're told – and has been situated here since the 1960s, when tea plants from an abandoned plantation elsewhere in the state were transported to their new home in Charleston. America's only tea plantation offers both loose-leaf and bagged varieties produced from a crop of *Camellia sinensis*, as well as a host of flavoured options, and does a roaring trade in tourism.

ALABAMA SWEET TEA
Serves four

'Sweet' being the operative word here, this one might rattle your fillings. But it's good to be authentic, and this is, after all, how they drink it in the hot and humid Deep South. Feel free to lighten the sugar load and enjoy a rather more muted version if you fear for your dental health.

Ingredients:
1.5 litres water
250 g caster sugar
Four orange pekoe teabags
A tray of ice cubes

Method:
- Place sugar and water in a pan and bring to the boil. Remove the pan from the heat, add teabags and steep for 5 minutes.
- Remove teabags and return pan to the heat, stirring the mixture until all the sugar has dissolved.
- Place the liquid into a large jug, add the ice cubes and stir. Once melted, top up with cold water and more ice cubes if you wish to consume immediately. Alternatively, leave to cool and store in the fridge.

SRI LANKA

Annual production:
330,000 tons

Main tea-growing regions:
Dimbula, Galle, Kandy, Nuwara Eliya, Ratnapura, Uva

Teas of note:
Black (Ceylon, Uva), white

- Sri Lanka's primary export was coffee until its entire crop was decimated by an agricultural parasite in 1869. The British introduced tea plants and the country has never looked back.

- As the fourth-largest producer of tea in the world, Sri Lanka is best known for its black tea Ceylon – the island's name until 1972.

- Any tea bearing the name 'Ceylon Tea' must have been grown and manufactured entirely in Sri Lanka, and must also adhere to strict regulations defined by the Sri Lanka Tea Board. To qualify for the Sri Lanka Lion logo, which appears on the country's flag, the tea must also have been packed in Sri Lanka.

- Each of Sri Lanka's main tea-growing regions exists in a different microclimate, with various weather patterns contributing to each tea's unique flavour.

TURKEY

Annual production:
225,000 tons

Main tea-growing regions:
Arakli, Fatsa, Karadere, Rize, Trabzon

Teas of note:
Black

- The Turks love their tea, so in 1938 they decided to grow the crop themselves. They now have around 60,000 small growers producing tea for domestic consumption.
- Turkish teas tend to be sweet and dark and are prepared using traditional methods (see Tea Drinking Around the World).

VIETNAM

Annual production:
216,900 tons

Main tea-growing regions:
Ha Giang, Phu Tho, Son La, Thai Nguyen, Tuyen Quang and Yen Bai

Teas of note:
Black, green

- Tea has been grown in Vietnam for over 3,000 years, although commercial production did not begin until the 1820s.

- Considered a delicacy, the most unusual of Vietnamese teas are the lotus-flavoured variety, made by leaving tea inside the blossoms of lotus flowers overnight, giving it a sweet, gentle flavour.

THANK GOD FOR TEA!
WHAT WOULD THE WORLD
DO WITHOUT TEA?

HOW DID IT EXIST? I AM
GLAD I WAS NOT BORN
BEFORE TEA.

Sydney Smith, *Lady Holland's Memoir*

OTHER TEA-PRODUCING COUNTRIES

1. Australia
2. Azerbaijan
3. Bolivia
4. Brazil
5. Burundi
6. Cameroon
7. the Democratic Republic of the Congo
8. Ecuador
9. Ethiopia
10. Georgia
11. Italy
12. Madagascar
13. Malaysia
14. Mauritius
15. Papua New Guinea

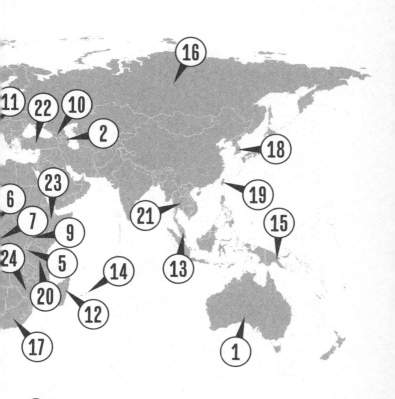

Peter was not very well during the evening. His mother put him to bed, and made some chamomile tea: 'One table-spoonful to be taken at bedtime.'

Beatrix Potter,
The Tale of Peter Rabbit

CHAPTER 4
A–Z OF TEA

*Honestly, if you're given the
choice between Armageddon
or tea, you don't say
'What kind of tea?'*
Neil Gaiman

ASSAM

Country of origin: India
In brief: Hailing from its namesake state in India, located south of the eastern Himalayas, Assam is found in most 'breakfast' teas. Second-flush Assam (picked during the second harvest of the year) is considered to be richer in flavour than first-flush and is given the nickname 'tippy tea' due to the golden tips of the leaves.
Taste: Malty, bold, strong
Serving suggestion: Milk and sugar, at your discretion

BLACK TEA

Country of origin: China
In brief: Black tea began its life in China and is a more oxidised version of the country's original green tea. The Chinese know it as 'red tea' and actually refer to fermented varieties as 'black tea'. Built to last, black tea can retain its flavour for several years – much longer than its former incarnation – which enables it to be transported great distances and stored for longer periods.
Taste: Strong, full-bodied
Serving suggestion: Milk and sugar, at your discretion

CEYLON

Country of origin: Sri Lanka
In brief: There are varieties of green and white Ceylon tea, but the black variety is the most lucrative. The tea is named after its home country, known until 1972 as Ceylon. Sri Lanka, which boasts myriad sub-regions across its relatively small tea-growing territory, offers dramatically different brews and is proud of its ability to produce such variety.
Taste: Full-bodied, aromatic
Serving suggestion: Milk and sugar, at your discretion

DARJEELING

Country of origin: India
In brief: The Darjeeling region is located at the base of the Himalayas in West Bengal in north-east India and produces what is frequently referred to as the 'Champagne of teas'. Darjeeling is unusual in that, unlike most Indian teas, it is produced from the Chinese variety of the *Camellia sinensis* plant.
Taste: Sweet, musky
Serving suggestion: Most add milk to Darjeeling, although tea purists claim this tends to mask the flavours, so why not add a slice of lemon instead? If you must add milk, be sure to pour cold milk into the cup ahead of the hot water to avoid spoiling.

THE TEAS OF SRI LANKA

The varied climate and terrain of Sri Lanka led to the production of a huge variety of teas. Here are a few of the key varieties:

Dimbula – the most famous Ceylon tea, with a light, bright colour, and a crisp, strong flavour.

Kenilworth – a variety with long, wiry leaves and an oaky taste.

Uva – a fine flavoured tea with a deep amber colour.

Saint James – a copper-coloured brew with a smooth taste.

Nuwara Eliya – light, delicate and fragrant, best enhanced with lemon rather than milk.

Nuwara Eliya Estate – a light, bright tea suited to being enjoyed with a small splash of milk.

**OH DARJEELING,
HOW I OOLONG FOR YOU!**

Anonymous

GREEN TEA

Country of origin: China
In brief: Green tea is the most ancient of teas. It is only lightly oxidised and is thought to offer various health benefits – with many proclaiming it the healthiest drink on the planet. Rich in antioxidants and polyphenols, which are known to help promote a healthy immune system and combat signs of skin ageing, as well as aiding digestion and improving brain function, polyphenols have been shown to inhibit cancer cell growth. Japan has long been a purveyor of green tea, taking the beverage very seriously indeed and building a way of life around it.
Taste: Bitter, grassy, fresh
Serving suggestion: Let boiling water cool in a container for a few minutes before adding to green tea leaves – otherwise the leaves will bruise and your brew may be a bit too much on the bitter side. Some people also like to add a slice of fresh apple to their just-brewed green tea.

ICED GREEN TEA
Serves four

This might look like something you'd serve up at a Halloween party (in, fact, I advise it), but it's an incredibly refreshing alternative to the classic iced tea.

Ingredients:
Eight green teabags or 8 tbsp loose green tea leaves
1.5 litres of water
1 apple, sliced
Plenty of ice cubes

Method:
- Simply boil 2 litres of water and brew the green tea for a few minutes. If you are using loose-leaf tea, be sure to strain the mixture.
- Either brew and set to one side to cool or, alternatively, cool the liquid with plenty of ice.
- Pour over more ice and add slices of apple to serve.

GYOKURO

Country of Origin: Japan
In brief: Gyokuro (literally 'jewel dew') is a green tea produced from a plant grown under cover for a short time, out of the sun, as opposed to sencha which is fully exposed. This process is referred to as *ooishita*, meaning 'under cover', and halts the growth of the young leaves so they become more concentrated in nutrients from the soil. Gyokuro is considered to be one of the highest-quality teas in Japan.
Taste: Smooth, rich, sweet aftertaste
Serving suggestion: Let boiling water cool a little before pouring it over the tea leaves; steep for a minute and a half, and serve.

HERBAL TEA

After being somewhat sniffed at by the UK masses for a considerable time, herbal teas have undergone something of a renaissance in recent years. With wide ranges readily available in all supermarkets and more proof of their various health-promoting properties, it seems more people are turning to these wonder teas all the time. Here are some of the most popular, along with some of their benefits:

- Blackberry leaves – High levels of vitamin C, good for sore throats and healthy immune systems
- Cardamom – Found to help treat indigestion, coughs and colds, and relieve the symptoms of PMT
- Chamomile – Calming, alleviates bloating, can be used as a sleep aid

- Dandelion – Cleanses the liver and helps with digestion
- Echinacea – A powerful preventative or cure for the common cold and generally good for an immune-system boost
- Ginger – Energising, anti-inflammatory, digestive aid
- Ginseng – Energising, good for the immune system, digestive aid, relief from PMT
- Hawthorn – Good for cardiovascular health and water retention
- Hibiscus – High in vitamin C and antioxidants, helps to lower blood pressure
- Lavender – Soothing, good for an upset stomach or lowering body temperature, can be used as a sleep aid

- Lemon balm – Calming for nerves or anxiety, can be used as a sleep aid
- Milk thistle – Cleanses the liver and helps with digestion
- Nettle – Found to help with symptoms of anaemia, arthritis, high blood pressure, congestion and kidney infection
- Peppermint – Digestive aid, good for headaches and sinus issues
- Rosehip – High in vitamin C, good for immune-system health and skin regeneration
- Rosemary – Digestive aid, found to help with gall bladder and liver problems, as well as coughs and mild asthma

Anne… was so pale and tragic at breakfast next morning that Marilla was alarmed and insisted on making her a cup of scorching ginger tea. Anne sipped it patiently, although she could not imagine what good ginger tea would do. Had it been some magic brew, potent to confer age and experience, Anne would have swallowed a quart of it without flinching.

Lucy Maud Montgomery, *Anne of Green Gables*

ICONIC BRANDING

Beloved British tea brand Twinings has sported the same logo on its products since 1787, making it the oldest commercial logo to have been in continuous use since it was designed.

Tea should be taken in solitude.

C. S. Lewis,
Surprised by Joy

KEEMUN

Country of origin: China

In brief: Keemun is a black tea hailing from south-western China, in the Anhui province. It is best known for its traditional production methods and is considered one of China's best teas. The manufacture of Keemun is a delicate process involving the drying of whole tea leaves, which have to be carefully handled, to result in thin, wiry strips from which you create your brew. With an aroma of orchids and roses, Keemun sits high up in the tea hierarchy.

Taste: Sweet, smoky, mellow

Serving suggestion: Brew with boiling water and add a little milk to enjoy its smoothness; however, if imbibing in China one tends to hold back the milk.

LAPSANG SOUCHONG

Country of origin: China

In brief: Another black tea that has been around for aeons, Lapsang Souchong is also unique in that, instead of being left to wither, its leaves are smoke-dried over burning pinewood to give it its signature smoky flavour. The term 'souchong' refers to the fourth and fifth leaves of the tea plant, which are further away than the sought-after bud. The smoke-drying process was devised as a way to treat the less-desirable leaves of the tea plant and, hey presto, one of the most popular teas was born.

Taste: Smoky, woody, earthy

Serving suggestion: Add boiling water and brew for 2 minutes or so. It's up to you whether you add milk; some tea aficionados find milky smoke to be an odd flavour indeed.

Tea is a divine herb.

Xu Guangqi

MATCHA

Country of Origin: Japan
In brief: Matcha is unlike other green teas in that it is always powdered and therefore ingested along with the water it has been stirred into. No mess, no fuss. As it's concentrated green tea, it carries a concentrated dose of the benefits (see Tea and Our Health). Matcha tea bushes are grown in the shade to maximise the leaves' nutrients.
Taste: Rich, vegetal, sweet aftertaste
Serving suggestion: Why not try an energising shot of matcha with your breakfast? Take half a teaspoon of the powder, add it to a small glass (a shot glass is best) and pour your drink of choice over it – orange juice, hot or cold milk, or hot or cold water work well. Grab a handheld milk frother or a fork, and whisk it up until the powder has dissolved. Then knock it back!

MATE TEA

Country of origin: Argentina
In brief: Mate teas are produced from the stems and leaves of the South American yerba mate plant. After much blanching, drying and ageing, the tea makes its way to the cup. Apparently, the most successful growing of the yerba mate plant occurs when the seeds have passed through the digestive tracts of certain birds.
Taste: Grassy, vegetal, herbal
Serving suggestion: If you have a gourd and a filtered straw knocking around, these seem to be the ultimate tools for consumption of mate tea; if not, grab a mug, add boiling water, steep for 5 minutes, strain and enjoy.

NILGIRI

Country of origin: India
In brief: Grown in the Blue Mountains, tea from Nilgiri accounts for around 25 per cent of India's crop. This type of black tea tends to be used in blends and creates an exceptionally fresh iced tea.
Taste: Punchy, fragrant, brisk
Serving suggestion: Either add hot water and a little milk, or cold-brew and serve with ice cubes and a slice of lemon.

OOLONG

Country of origin: China
In brief: There are many different types of oolong and, unlike most other teas, they can be infused several times and still produce a decent cupful. Tea leaves are semi-oxidised and, depending on the cultivars, can produce a fresh, woody or sweet and fruity taste when infused.
Taste: Oolong teas are often flavoured, and can be floral or fruity.
Serving suggestion: Rinse the leaves first to help them unfurl freely; add hot water and enjoy.

TEA LEAVES SHOULD HAVE
FOLDS LIKE THE LEATHER BOOTS
OF TARTAR HORSEMEN AND
CURLS LIKE THE DEWLAPS OF
A MIGHTY OX; THEY SHOULD
BE MOIST AND SOFT TO THE
TOUCH, LIKE THE EARTH
FRESHLY SWEPT BY RAIN.

Lu Yu

PU-ERH

Country of origin: China

In brief: Grown in the Yunnan province in south-west China, Pu-erh tea leaves are produced using fermentation and ageing methods, and are said to have many health-giving properties. Thought to help with weight loss, stomach upset and digestion, as well as lowering cholesterol, the dark Pu-erh tea leaves can be aged for up to a year to reach their optimum flavour.

Taste: Earthy, woody

Serving suggestion: Rinse the leaves to wash away impurities, and add hot water; the hotter the water, the stronger your brew. Steep for 2 minutes and enjoy.

ROOIBOS

Country of origin: South Africa
In brief: Also known as 'redbush tea', this South African 'tea' has risen in popularity in recent years, marketed as a caffeine-free alternative to much-loved 'breakfast tea'. It is also rich in antioxidants, which scores big points with health-conscious tea drinkers. Grown off the Western Cape, the Rooibos plant is a shrub-like member of the legume family, so is unrelated to the *Camellia sinensis*.
Taste: Refreshing, lightly nutty
Serving suggestion: Add hot water and serve with a little milk or a slice of lemon.

SENCHA

Country of Origin: Japan
In brief: Sencha is king of the green teas in Japan in terms of consumption and makes up around 80 per cent of the country's green tea production. These long, narrow tea leaves unfurl in the bottom of your cup to create a miniature garden and a delectable, dark and intense brew.
Taste: Grassy, robust, sweet
Serving suggestion: Let boiling water cool for a few minutes before pouring it over the leaves. Then steep for at least 2 minutes; the darker your cup of tea, the more intense.

I am in no way
interested in
immortality, but only
in the taste of tea.

Lu T'ung

SIKKIM

Country of origin: India

In brief: Grown in north-eastern India, nestled between Bhutan and Nepal, Sikkim is quite close in taste to Darjeeling, but boasts a bit more body. Due to the small scale of production, Sikkim is one of the lesser-known teas here, so you might not find it as readily on the supermarket shelves, but tea adventurers are advised to seek it out and give it a whirl.

Taste: Malty, light, sweet

Serving suggestion: Critics are divided as to whether one should add milk, so try both and see what you prefer.

The Temi Tea Garden, established in 1969, is the only tea plantation in the Sikkim province of India. Although a mere 180 acres in size, the tea garden produces some of the best tea in the world, and its products are always in high demand when traded at the Kolkata Tea Auction Centre.

WHITE TEA

Country of origin: China

In brief: White tea is produced using the buds of the tea plant, which makes for a sweet and delicate brew. Primarily grown in the Fujian and Zhejiang provinces of China, the buds are generally only withered for a short time in natural sunlight before being lightly processed, leading to a tea that has only been very briefly tampered with.

Taste: Sweet, light, elegant

Serving suggestion: Infuse in a small amount of water for a few minutes to release the subtle flavours, and then strain and infuse again.

TOP TIP

Raise a handful of tea leaves to your nose and inhale their aroma before steeping; once brewed and cooled a little, be sure to slurp your tea to allow the full flavour to cover your tongue.

YELLOW TEA

Country of origin: China

In brief: Yellow tea is very similar to green tea, although the drying stage of production is lengthier. Allowing the damp tea leaves to mellow somewhat lends it quite a different taste and aroma to its green and white counterparts, the aim originally being to remove the grassiness of green tea, making it easier on the stomach, without losing its health benefits. Yellow teas are quite rare and are generally produced in small quantities.

Taste: Smooth, mild

Serving suggestion: Let boiling water cool in an open container for a few minutes before adding it to the tea leaves.

Tea is quiet and our thirst for tea is never far from our craving for beauty.

James Norwood Pratt

YUNNAN (ALSO KNOWN AS DIANHONG)

Country of origin: China

In brief: Grown just north of Vietnam in south-western China, Yunnan tea is considered to be a gourmet offering in its home nation and is produced using tea leaves with golden tips. The leaves are traditionally fermented with longan fruit, lychee and rose to create sweet and delicate flavours, but the mass-produced varieties that make it to our shores tend to be nutty and peppery in taste.

Taste: Peppery, rich, nutty

Serving suggestion: Steep in boiling water for 3 minutes or so and add a splash of milk.

Blooming and treasure teas should be imbibed from a transparent vessel or brewed in a glass teapot. Dried flowers are wrapped in green tea leaves and hand-sewn into place, so that a charming miniature ornamental garden delicately unfolds in your teacup.

TASTING TEA

Why not try a few of the teas described in this chapter, and use the table on the following pages to record your notes?

Here are some words used by professional tea tasters when describing tea:

You are bound to come up with more when you start tasting! Just as with wine-tasting, the world of tea-tasting allows your imagination to soar as your palate becomes more and more attuned to the subtle variations of flavour on offer.

TEA: A MISCELLANY

Tea type	Brand	Loose tea or teabag?	Brewing time	Served with milk/lemon/sugar/honey/other?

Tasting notes

**TEA! BLESS ORDINARY EVERYDAY
AFTERNOON TEA!**

Agatha Christie

CHAPTER 5

TEA DRINKING AROUND THE WORLD

There is something in the nature of tea that leads us into a world of quiet contemplation of life.

Lin Yutang

Always been a milk, two sugars type of tea drinker? Why not expand your horizons and try some more exotic serves? Here's how they do it elsewhere around the globe.

ARGENTINA

Argentina is a substantial grower of black teas – the majority of which are exported to the USA and used in blends and iced teas – but it's mate tea for which the country is best known. Not strictly a tea, as there is no involvement of the *Camellia sinensis*, mate tea, derived from the broom-like yerba mate plant and blended with spices or fruit, is considered the national brew.

CHINA

We're all aware by now that tea was born in China and was originally adopted for medicinal purposes, but how is it drunk there today? Considering the country's sheer size, it is perhaps not surprising that the way the Chinese prepare and drink their tea varies from region to region. Green tea is preferred in China but some ferment it in bamboo, while others chew the leaves as a snack, and many infuse it with sugar and walnuts. However, the most common tea-drinking practice involves simply placing some tea leaves into a cup and, without pomp and circumstance, submerging them in boiling water.

Water is the mother of tea, a teapot its father, and fire the teacher.

Chinese proverb

HONG KONG

Now here's an unusual one… Hong Kong dwellers prefer a very milky black tea-infused beverage, using evaporated or condensed milk, which is known throughout the region as 'pantyhose milk tea'. The name is derived from the way the drink is prepared, which involves straining it through a type of sackcloth that bears some resemblance to a stocking. Ah, it all makes sense now.

INDIA

As well as being the second-largest producer of tea in the world, India's population drinks traditional masala chai by the absolute bucketload. Strong tea is mixed with spices such as cardamom pods, cinnamon sticks, cloves, ginger and peppercorns, and boiled in milk. The brew is often bought from street vendors and served in a disposable earthenware bowl that can be easily discarded once drained. In recent years, chai tea has become increasingly popular across the globe and is often marketed as 'tea latte' in the US.

Drinking a daily cup of tea

will surely starve

the apothecary.

Chinese proverb

CHAI SPICED TEA
Serves two

Evoke the heady aromas of Indian street markets with this hot, sweet and sumptuous beverage.

Ingredients:
3 tsp loose-leaf black tea
Four whole cardamom pods
Four whole cloves
Four whole black peppercorns
450 ml water
225 ml milk
Sugar, to taste
One stick cinnamon, to serve

Method:
- Place the water in a pan over a medium heat and, while that's heating, place the spices in a bowl and bruise gently with a spoon.
- Add the spices to the water and simmer for 10 minutes, then add the milk and simmer for a further 2 minutes.
- Serve with a cinnamon stick and add sugar to taste.

TEA TRADITION

In Sri Lanka tea is traditionally drunk at lunchtime and throughout the afternoon, and is served in 'hoppers', a type of rice-flour pancake made with coconut milk and moulded into a bowl shape to act as a tea vessel.

*Each cup of tea represents
an imaginary voyage.*

Catherine Douzel

JAPAN

Green tea is favoured in Japan – the nation that quite possibly takes the beverage the most seriously of all, elevating it to a way of life. The traditional Japanese tea ceremony, or the 'Way of Tea', is a Zen Buddhist-inspired ritual that involves great attention to detail in the way the loose tea is scooped, the water boiled and the teacup handled. People have written theses on the detail and meaning of each intricate stage and action involved in the ceremony, and it can often take years of training to master the art of its performance. Therefore, the steps outlined below are a somewhat pared-down version.

If man has no tea in him, he is incapable of understanding truth and beauty.

Japanese proverb

JAPANESE TEA CEREMONY: STEP BY STEP

Equipment needed: Matcha green tea powder, a traditional tea bowl (*tenmoku chawan*), tea scoop (*chashaku*), bamboo whisk (*chasen*), a kettle or pan in which to boil water.

- Guests often wait in a different room from where the ceremony will take place and are required to walk across moist ground (*roji*), in order to symbolically purify themselves prior to the ceremony. To further purify themselves, guests then wash their hands and mouth in a stone basin (*tsukabi*).

- The host of the tea ceremony receives the guests through a short door, so they have to bow upon entering the room. The host bows silently to each guest.

- An informal ceremony might see guests served with a light sweet snack (*wagashi*), whereas in a more formal situation a three-course meal would be served.

- In preparation, the equipment is cleaned with water brought to the boil and then cooled. The host of the tea ceremony will perform this cleaning task with graceful, sweeping movements.

- Three scoops of matcha per guest are placed in the tea bowl, hot water is ladled into the bowl and the whisk is used to mix the tea into the water.

- The host will hand the tea to the first guest, who will admire the liquid and rotate the bowl once, before taking a sip, wiping the rim and passing it to the next guest. This is repeated until each guest has taken a drink from the bowl.

- Once all guests have taken a drink, the host empties the tea bowl and cleans all the equipment once again while the guests watch. Then the guests exit the ceremony room.

MOROCCO

Moroccans started drinking mint tea in the 1800s and its popularity shows few signs of waning. Tea is prepared in various different ways, according to region, and is widely considered the national drink. Moroccan tea drinkers favour a metal teapot, to which they add mint and sugar (and absinthe on special occasions), and serve their infusion in glasses, always poured with ceremony from a great height to create froth and aerate the liquid. The tea is then poured back into the pot to ensure an even mix before being returned to the glasses for consumption.

PAKISTAN

Pakistanis favour both black and green teas, but what sets them apart from other tea-loving nations (Pakistan is the third-largest importer of tea in the world) is their traditional Kashmir pink noon chai tea, prepared with milk, almonds, pistachios and spices. And if their huge imports weren't enough proof of their dedication to tea, one only has to look at Pakistan's state emblem, where a tea bush takes pride of place.

*The hostess, with freshly arranged coiffure
and freshened face, walked in at one
door and her guests at the other door
of the drawing room, a large room with
dark walls, downy rugs, and a brightly
lighted table, gleaming with the light
of candles, white cloth, silver samovar,
and transparent china tea things.*

Leo Tolstoy, *Anna Karenina*

RUSSIA

Tea is so important to the Russians that prisoners receive a regular ration as a basic requirement. In Russia tea is also available pretty much on tap everywhere, via a samovar – a sometimes grand appliance that heats water via a charcoal fire in its base to keep a good supply at the ready whenever the need for tea arises. A strong, black tea concentrate, *zavarka*, is prepared, to which hot water is added from the samovar. The drinker can then control the intensity of their brew by adding more or less water, which is nearly always sweetened. The samovar has also been adopted by Iran, Turkey and Afghanistan.

RUSSIAN TEA
Serves two

You may not have the fancy samovar that is part and parcel of the Russian tea-drinking repertoire, but that doesn't mean you can't enjoy the warming flavours this delectable brew offers.

Ingredients:
2 tsp black tea leaves
2 tsp sugar
20 ml orange juice
20 ml pineapple juice
A squirt of lemon juice
A few cloves

Method:
- Add 500 ml of boiling water to the tea leaves and steep for a couple of minutes.
- Strain the tea into a pan and add the rest of the ingredients. Bring to the boil, stirring in the sugar, then leave to simmer for half an hour.
- Strain into a teapot and enjoy the wonderful aromas.

TAIWAN

It's likely that in recent years you've spotted someone walking down the street drinking what looks like an iced coffee with a helping of eyeballs nestled at the bottom. Those 'eyeballs' are actually tapioca pearls and that 'iced coffee' is known as bubble tea. In Taiwan it has been all about bubble tea since the 1980s, when what at first seemed like a passing fad refused to disappear. Bubble teas generally consist of a tea base with added fruit juice and milk – oh, and 'eyeballs' for good measure. In the 2000s the craze went positively global.

TIBET

Tibetans favour a kind of salty butter tea, or *po cha*, consisting of black tea brewed with water, goat's milk, yak butter and salt. Served in wooden bowls, the beverage symbolises hospitality of the highest order as well as being vital to the daily routine of Tibetans, as the combination of tea and salty fat is considered an ideal energy booster for the high altitude of the Himalayas.

TURKEY

Although Turkey's method of preparing coffee is 'borrowed' by restaurants all over the world, it is black tea that is more widely consumed throughout the country. Turks use a sort of double-decker teapot, which sees tea brewed in the top deck and water heated in the bottom, to create a strong brew that can be weakened with the addition of water. No one takes milk, but everyone takes sugar. Turkish tea is generally brewed for much longer than most other teas and is served in tall tulip-shaped glasses.

TIME FOR TEA

The Duchess of Bedford is widely credited with introducing the ritual of afternoon tea in 1840, when people generally ate only two meals a day – breakfast and dinner. She began to notice a 'sinking feeling' around 4 p.m. and so took to having tea accompanied by a light snack.

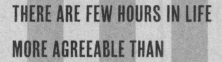

THERE ARE FEW HOURS IN LIFE
MORE AGREEABLE THAN

THE HOUR DEDICATED TO
THE CEREMONY KNOWN
AS AFTERNOON TEA.

Henry James,
The Portrait of a Lady

UNITED KINGDOM

Black tea is the tipple of choice in the UK, although the health-chasing population are increasingly looking to green tea for both its caffeine and antioxidant properties. There is no right or wrong time of day for tea in the UK: tea with breakfast, lunch, dinner, in-between at any hour and in bed at either end of the day are all considered perfectly acceptable and not out of the ordinary. Most Brits also like to drink tea in the afternoon with a slab of cake and many UK eateries have made a living from the nation's sweet tooth, with several towers of sandwiches, scones and other treats accompanied by a brew considered an acceptable way to spend an afternoon.

Tea had come as a deliverer to a land that called for deliverance; a land... of grey skies and harsh winds; of strong-nerved, stout-purposed, slow-thinking men and women... a land of firesides that were waiting, waiting for the bubbling kettle and the fragrant breath of tea.

Agnes Repplier, *To Think of Tea!*

HIGH TEA V LOW TEA

High tea is often misconstrued as an incredibly lavish affair with sumptuous cakes and plenty of fine-quality tea, but the term actually originates from the Victorian era and is how the British working classes would refer to their evening meal at their 'high table' after an honest day's slog. Afternoon tea, much as the Duchess of Bedford might take, was referred to as 'low tea' simply because one might sit in an armchair with the tea served at a side table that might be rather low.

My hour for tea is half-past five, and my buttered toast waits for nobody.

Wilkie Collins

USA

Being a vast land of many climates, the tea-drinking habits of Americans understandably vary from coast to coast, time zone to time zone, but for the most part the coffee-loving Land of the Free is still incredibly loyal to its regular cup of joe.

When it comes to tea, as a general rule, Americans tend not to opt for the warm variety, with 85 per cent of the country's tea consumption involving a whole load of ice, although hot tea drinking is on the rise. In the south you'll find jaw-achingly sweet iced tea is the order of the day.

'I can just imagine myself sitting down at the head of the table and pouring out the tea,' said Anne, shutting her eyes ecstatically. 'And asking Diana if she takes sugar! I know she doesn't but of course I'll ask her just as if I didn't know. And then pressing her to take another piece of fruit cake and another helping of preserves. Oh, Marilla, it's a wonderful sensation just to think of it.'

Lucy Maud Montgomery, *Anne of Green Gables*

Iced tea is too pure…
not to have been
invented as soon
as tea, ice, and hot
weather crossed paths.

John Egerton

CHAPTER 6

HOW DO YOU DRINK YOURS?

A Proper Tea is much nicer than a Very Nearly Tea, which is one you forget about afterwards.

A. A. Milne

Do your colleagues bemoan the colour, flavour, strength, intensity or temperature of your lovingly crafted brew? Has anyone rudely offered you a Pantone card to refer to the next time you're on tea duty? There's certainly no getting around the fact that tea connoisseurs know how they take theirs and tend to think anything other than their preferred serve is below par. Therefore, how to brew the perfect cup of tea is the subject of much debate – and debate it we do.

Indeed, madam, your ladyship is very sparing of your tea: I protest, the last I took was no more than water bewitch'd.

Jonathan Swift

THE SCIENCE OF BREWING

In 2011, Cravendale Milk commissioned research into how one might concoct a better brew. Scientists at the University of Northumbria concluded a 2-minute wait after adding boiling water to your teabag will bring about the most desired tea strength and, once milk has been added, the tea should be left to sit for 6 minutes before consumption to reach its optimum temperature and ultimate flavour potential.

GOT MILK?

The debate over when to add milk to your tea – before or after the water, or before or after steeping – has long been raging. Some experts say adding the milk first is nothing but a cultural oddity, having no impact whatsoever on taste, while others claim that subjecting milk to high temperatures (i.e. boiling water straight from the kettle) can alter the taste by degrading the milk proteins and thus not producing the freshest cup of tea possible.

I rang for the tea, and the waiter, reappearing with his magic clew, brought in by degrees some fifty adjuncts to that refreshment, but of tea not a glimpse... After a prolonged absence at this stage of the entertainment, he at length came back with a casket of precious appearance containing twigs. These I steeped in hot water, and so from the whole of these appliances extracted one cup of I don't know what for Estella.

Charles Dickens, *Great Expectations*

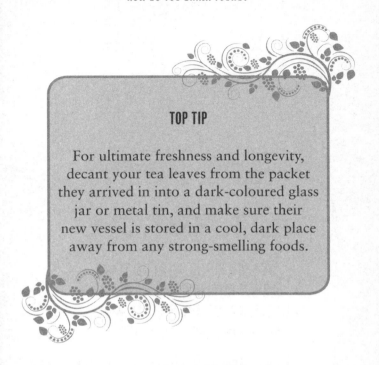

TOP TIP

For ultimate freshness and longevity, decant your tea leaves from the packet they arrived in into a dark-coloured glass jar or metal tin, and make sure their new vessel is stored in a cool, dark place away from any strong-smelling foods.

SOME LIKE IT HOT – BUT NOT TOO HOT

Most people make tea with water that has just boiled, but if you take the water off the heat just before it reaches a rolling boil (when small bubbles appear at the sides of the kettle), the resulting tea will be sweeter and less astringent. Some types of tea don't even like their water to be quite this hot: for camomile tea, 90°C is just right; oolongs prefer around 85°C; and fine white and green teas are best brewed with water at 70°C.

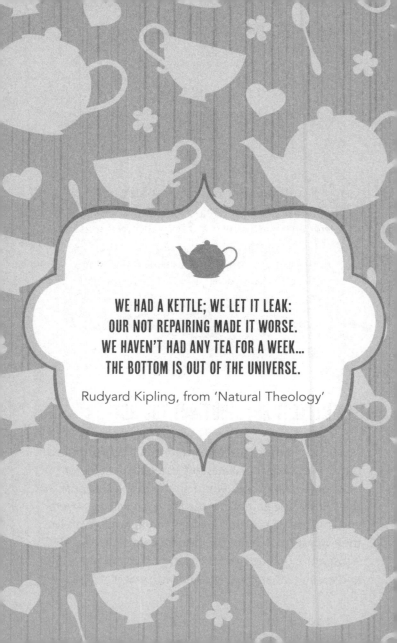

WE HAD A KETTLE; WE LET IT LEAK:
OUR NOT REPAIRING MADE IT WORSE.
WE HAVEN'T HAD ANY TEA FOR A WEEK...
THE BOTTOM IS OUT OF THE UNIVERSE.

Rudyard Kipling, from 'Natural Theology'

GEORGE ORWELL'S TEA RULES

George Orwell had 11 rules when it came to tea brewing, every one of which, he said, should be regarded as 'golden'. He was very particular indeed when it came to his breakfast brew, and his rules, published in his essay 'A Nice Cup of Tea' which featured in the *Evening Standard* in 1946, went something like this:

1. The tea should always be Indian or 'Ceylonese' (from Sri Lanka) as, according to George, 'there is not much stimulation' in Chinese tea.

2. The tea should always be prepared in a teapot 'made of china or earthenware'. 'Silver or Britanniaware teapots produce inferior tea and enamel pots are worse,' insists George, 'though curiously enough a pewter teapot is not so bad.'

3. Make sure you warm the pot beforehand. George suggests 'placing it on the hob' rather than 'swilling it out with hot water'; however, if you value your teapot, the latter might be preferable.

4. Tea should always be served strong. George admits post-war rationing is an issue but maintains that 'one strong cup of tea is better than twenty weak ones'. 'All true tea lovers not only like their tea strong,' he says, 'but like it a little stronger with each year that passes – a fact which is recognised in the extra ration issued to old-age pensioners.'

5. George insists that tea leaves should always be placed directly into the teapot and there should be absolutely no faffing about with teabags and strainers. 'One can swallow tea leaves in considerable quantities without ill effect, and if the tea is not loose in the pot it never infuses properly.'

6. The teapot should be taken to the kettle rather than the other way around, to ensure the correct temperature of the water, which 'should be actually boiling at the moment of impact'.

7. The next stage should be not just to stir your tea but to 'give the pot a good shake' and then allow time for the leaves to settle.

8. The tea-drinking vessel is very important to George, who insists on 'the cylindrical type of cup, not the flat, shallow type', which, George says, leads one's tea to be 'half cold before one has well started on it'.

9. Cream atop your bottle of milk is not as great an issue as it once was, but George reminds the reader to remove it before using milk for tea. 'Milk that is too creamy always gives tea sickly taste,' he says. That would make him a fan of green or even red top, then, were he still with us.

10. Tea comes first – straight into the cup – and should be followed by the milk, *NOT the other way around*, quite simply because, 'by putting the tea in first and stirring as one pours, one can exactly regulate the amount of milk, whereas one is liable to put in too much milk if one does it the other way round.'

11. Do not add sugar, stresses George. I repeat, do not add sugar. Poor George admits he is in the minority, but feels very strongly indeed that sugar does nothing but ruin his favourite tipple. 'How can you call yourself a true tea lover if you destroy the flavour of your tea by putting sugar in it? It would be equally reasonable to put in pepper or salt.' Steady on, George.

A dreadful controversy has broken out in Bath, whether tea is most effectually sweetened by lump or pounded sugar.

Saba Holland, *A Memoir of the Reverend Sydney Smith*

LOOSE TEA VERSUS THE TEABAG

The pros and cons of the hassle-free paper tea sack, one of the wonders of the modern age, and true tea leaves in their natural, unrestricted state has been hotly debated for a long time. But surely both have a place in our day-to-day, tea-loving routine?

CAFFEINE COUNT

The caffeine content of tea depends on the amount of tea leaves you use and the brewing time, but a standard teabag-made cup contains at least half the amount of caffeine compared with an average cup of coffee. Decaffeinated tea is obtained by washing the leaves in an organic solvent in the final stages of the production process.

LOOSE TEA LEAVES

Pros
- There is an almost endless choice of flavours, and you have the freedom to create your own blends.
- You are in control of how much tea you add to the pot.
- Should you wish to perform a tea ceremony one day, you would be able to practise the all-important art of measuring.

Cons
- The equipment needed is rather more high maintenance than a teabag and a cup.
- Loose-leaf tea brewing is something of an art and, as with any art, your time and patience are required.
- Oh what a mess.

TEABAGS

Pros

- Oh, the convenience – you could even keep your favourite teabag in your pocket in case of an emergency and it wouldn't spill.
- No measuring necessary – one bag does it unless you're doing a tea round.
- No mess, no hassle.

Cons

- Flavours aren't always allowed to reach their full potential.
- Teabags don't tend to age as well as loose-leaf teas.
- There isn't, by any stretch, as wide a selection of teas available in bag as out.

TEA – THE CUPS
THAT CHEER

BUT NOT INEBRIATE.

William Cowper

WATCH YOUR WATER

You might not realise it, but the water you use to make your tea can have quite an effect on its flavour. Tea brewed from the water from one tap can taste flat and lifeless, while it can be incredibly bright and fresh when brewed from the water from a different location. Experts recommend filtering your water before you fill the kettle for the ultimate cup of tea – especially so if you live in a hard-water area, as the high levels of calcium tend to supress the flavours in your brew.

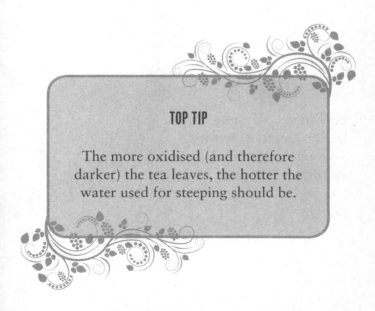

TOP TIP

The more oxidised (and therefore darker) the tea leaves, the hotter the water used for steeping should be.

WHEN SHOULD YOU DRINK YOURS?

Elevenses – Teas such as Lapsang Souchong or an Earl Grey blend work well to provide a dose of mid-morning caffeine and rich and smoky or delicate and fragrant flavours respectively.

Breakfast – Opt for English Breakfast/Assam for a morning dose of caffeine and plenty of flavour.

Lunchtime – If you fancy washing down your lunch with a cup of tea, why not try a herbal tea that aids digestion, such as peppermint.

Afternoon – Lighter teas are recommended as the day goes on, so try something soothing such as green tea or Darjeeling, or the trusty 'afternoon tea'.

Evening – As well as peppermint, dandelion and ginger teas, both green and white teas are good palate cleansers and will help with digestion after dinner.

EARL GREY MAR-TEA-NI
Serves one

Earl Grey lovers of the world, take note – you will like this cocktail *a lot*. We therefore advise caution when dipping one's toe into the realms of tea-inspired alcoholic drinks, lest you start to feel it might be an acceptable accompaniment to a bowl of cornflakes.

Ingredients:
50 ml gin
35 ml strong cold Earl Grey tea
20 ml lemon juice
12 ½ ml sugar syrup
½ an egg white
Lemon peel and wedges, to garnish

Method:
- Prepare the Earl Grey tea in advance as it needs to be completely cool and preferably chilled when it comes to constructing this cocktail.
- Place all ingredients into an ice-filled cocktail shaker and give it a good rattle. Strain into a Martini glass, run a lemon wedge around the rim and garnish with a twist of peel or float a lemon wedge on top.

COLD BREWING

It's not all about preparing tea to drink steaming from a mug; there's a knack to concocting the perfect iced tea, too, though admittedly cold brewing tends to be a little more popular in countries that can actually boast a decent stretch of summer!

Cold brewing is also a great way to extract maximum flavour from loose tea leaves, as iced tea made in this way is brewed for longer and therefore benefits from more of the tea leaves' natural goodness.

Simply measure out 1 tsp of loose-leaf black tea per glass, place in an infuser and pour your desired amount of room-temperature water through the tea leaves. Leave in the fridge for around 6 hours, or overnight, serve with slices of lemon and there you have it – a rather different flavour of iced tea, with not a hint of bitterness in sight.

Love and scandal
are the best
sweeteners of tea.

Henry Fielding,
Love in Several Masques

CHAPTER 7
RECIPES

*Ecstasy is a glass
full of tea and a
piece of sugar
in the mouth.*

Alexander Pushkin

SOMETHING SWEET

GREEN TEA CUPCAKES

Not only do these look fantastic, but the subtle green tea flavour is quite delicious, and there aren't many cakes you can claim are laced with health-giving properties. Oh, go on, have another.

Serves 12

INGREDIENTS:

For the cupcakes:
   150 ml milk
   225 g granulated sugar
   110 g unsalted butter
   250 g self-raising flour
   Three green teabags
   3 tsp green tea powder (matcha)
   Two large eggs

For the icing:
   500 g icing sugar
   115 g unsalted butter
   60 ml milk
   1 tsp vanilla extract
   1 tsp green tea powder (matcha)

METHOD:

- Bring the milk almost to the boil, remove from heat and add the teabags. Cover and leave for at least 30 minutes. When ready to press on, preheat oven to 180ºC (or 160ºC for a fan oven). Remove teabags from milk, give them a good squeeze, and stir in the green tea powder.

- Mix the butter and sugar into a creamy consistency and add the eggs. Sift the flour into the bowl a bit at a time, adding small amounts of the milk in-between to keep the mixture from drying out.

- Divide the mixture between 12 paper cases in a muffin tin and bake for around 25 minutes. Leave to cool and get on with the icing.

- To make the icing, beat together the milk, butter, vanilla extract and half the icing sugar until smooth. Add the rest of the icing sugar and the green tea powder gradually until creamy. Make sure the cupcakes are completely cool and then ice, dusting with a little green tea powder.

FRUITY TEA LOAF

A cup of tea consumed around 4 p.m. just wouldn't be the same without a cakey accompaniment, and what better than a tea-inspired slice of some such to complement your brew?

Serves ten

INGREDIENTS:

350 g mixed dried fruit of your choice
50 g Demerara sugar
50 g soft brown sugar
150 ml cold tea
225 g self-raising flour
One large egg

METHOD:

- Stir the dried fruit, sugar and tea into a bowl, cover and leave overnight in a cool, dark place.

- When you're ready to start baking, preheat the oven to 200ºC (or 180ºC for a fan oven), grease a 23 x 13 cm loaf tin and line with baking paper.

- Beat the egg and add it to the dried fruit mixture along with the flour. Mix well and pour into the tin.

- Bake for 35–40 minutes; the loaf is ready when an inserted skewer comes out clean. Leave on a wire rack to cool.

'Tea' to the English is really a picnic indoors.

Alice Walker

EARL GREY AND LAVENDER ICE CREAM

Move over, coffee ice cream, there's a new caffeine-laced frosty sheriff in town. You'll want to make this stuff in double batches, as it won't last long.

Serves four

INGREDIENTS:

250 ml double cream
250 ml full-fat milk
75 g caster sugar
4 heaped tsp Earl Grey loose leaves
Five large egg yolks
1 tsp fresh lavender, chopped

METHOD:

- Mix the cream and milk together and bring to the boil over a medium heat.

- Whisk the eggs and sugar together until smooth and then add the milk/cream mixture. Stir in the tea leaves and the lavender and leave to settle for half an hour.

- Sieve the mixture and allow it to cool.

- Once cooled, freeze the mixture in a plastic container for 2 hours. Then remove from freezer and blend in a food processor for a few minutes. Return to freezer for 2 further hours before serving.

I take pleasure in tea, appreciating it with my spirit and therefore cannot explain why.

Sen Joo

SHOULD I, AFTER TEA AND CAKES AND ICES,
HAVE THE STRENGTH TO FORCE
THE MOMENT TO ITS CRISIS?

T. S. Eliot

THE PERFECT ACCOMPANIMENTS

SCONES

For the perfect cream tea, these scones, served with clotted cream and jam, are hard to beat. They are best eaten fresh from the oven – but they taste so good that they're unlikely to be around for long anyway!

Makes 8–12

INGREDIENTS:

For the scones:
   225 g self-raising flour
   1 tsp baking powder
   2 tbsp caster sugar
   50 g butter, diced
   One egg, beaten
   90 ml milk

To serve:
   Clotted cream
   Strawberry jam

METHOD:

- Preheat the oven to 200°C. Line a baking tray with baking paper.

- In a large bowl, combine the flour, baking powder and sugar. Rub in the butter until the mixture resembles breadcrumbs.

- Make a well in the centre and add the egg and milk, leaving a small amount of the milk aside. Stir the mixture together and knead on a lightly floured work surface until the dough is smooth.

- Press out the dough to 2½ cm thick, and cut into rounds using a biscuit cutter. Place on the baking tray and brush the tops with the leftover milk to glaze.

- Bake for 10–12 minutes, or until golden brown.

- Place on a wire rack to cool. Serve with clotted cream and strawberry jam.

SHORTBREAD FINGERS

These melt-in-your-mouth treats are absolute simplicity to make, but taste utterly heavenly. They are perfect for nibbling at teatime – in fact, these fingers are so delicious that you won't be able to keep your hands off them.

Makes 20

INGREDIENTS:

125 g butter
55 g caster sugar, plus extra for sprinkling
180 g plain flour

METHOD:

- Heat the oven to 190°C. Line a baking tray with baking paper.

- Beat the butter and the sugar together in a bowl until smooth, then add the flour, stirring to form a paste.

- Place on a lightly floured work surface and gently roll out the paste to approx. 1 cm thick.

- Cut into fingers and place on the tray. Sprinkle with sugar and chill in the fridge for 20 minutes.
- Bake in the oven for 15–20 minutes, or until light golden brown.

Shortbread has beneficial effects on the soul.

Lucy Ellmann

A TOUCH OF THE SAVOURY

TEA-SMOKED MACKEREL

This is a great way to create smoked flavours in the comfort of your own home, but it can get very smoky indeed. Make sure an extractor fan is on or a nearby window can be cranked open. Serve your mackerel fillets with a pile of green beans and oven-roasted cherry tomatoes.

Serves four

INGREDIENTS:

Eight mackerel fillets
100 g white rice
100 g Demerara sugar
5 tsp black tea (or experiment with different varieties/blends)
Salt and pepper

METHOD:

- Grease a wire cooling rack with a little oil and line up the mackerel fillets on the top; add a dusting of salt and pepper.

- Take a wok and line it with foil. Then, after mixing the uncooked rice, sugar and tea, add them to the bottom of the pan. Place over a high heat.

- Once the mixture begins to smoke, place the cooling rack over the pan and turn off the heat. Leave to cook slowly for around 15 minutes as the mixture in the pan cools down.

For a healthy salad dressing with a difference, mix together matcha green tea powder, oil, garlic, lemon juice, and salt and pepper to taste, and pour over hearty salads.

Add a teaspoon of strong black tea to gravies, soups and stews to give them a kick.

LAPSANG SOUCHONG MARBLED QUAIL EGGS

This Chinese classic is easy to prepare and looks quite stunning – perfect nibbles to impress dinner guests.

Makes 12

INGREDIENTS:

12 quail eggs
Four Lapsang Souchong teabags
One star anise
1 tsp black peppercorns
Salt

METHOD:

- Cover the eggs with water and bring to the boil. Take the pan from the heat and leave to stand for around 5 minutes. Add the salt to the water.

- Remove the eggs and lightly tap all over to crack the shells. Pour the water from the pan into a bowl, place the eggs in the bowl with t h e rest of the ingredients and, when cooled, place in the fridge.

- Leave in the fridge for several hours or overnight; peel and serve.

SWEET TEA CHICKEN

This recipe is perfect for when you have the family round for dinner, and so simple too. The dish's delicate but moreish flavours will have everyone asking for the secret ingredient – you might want to give them a hint by serving it with a pot of tea!

Serves four

INGREDIENTS:

Three black teabags
120 g brown sugar
60 g salt
One onion, sliced
One lemon, sliced
Three garlic cloves, sliced
Two sprigs rosemary
1 tbsp cracked black pepper
2 handfuls of ice cubes
Four chicken breasts

METHOD:

- Boil 500 ml of water and steep the teabags for 10 minutes. Remove pan from heat.

- Dissolve the sugar and salt in the tea and add the onion, lemon, garlic and rosemary. Then add the ice cubes and cool the mixture.

- Marinate the chicken in the mixture overnight. Once marinated, grill the chicken and serve on a bed of leaves or with green vegetables.

Cookery is become an art, a noble science: cooks are gentlemen.

Robert Burton, *The Anatomy of Melancholy*

NOW FOR SOMETHING A BIT DIFFERENT...

Rice tea is considered a delicacy in China and is as easy as pie to brew at home. Simply toast a couple of tablespoons of rice in a pan until browned, add a litre of water and keep on the heat for a minute or so. Steep for a few minutes more and then strain into mugs – delicious.

Ginger tea is also an easy one to prepare yourself and tastes so much fresher than the shop-bought bagged variety. Peel a 5 cm piece of ginger root and chop into a pan of boiling water – about 2 litres should do it. Cover the pan and leave on a high heat for around half an hour. Reduce the heat a little, uncover and leave on the heat for a further 15 minutes. Strain into mugs and enjoy – ideal when in need of an energy boost or feeling the first sniffles of a winter cold.

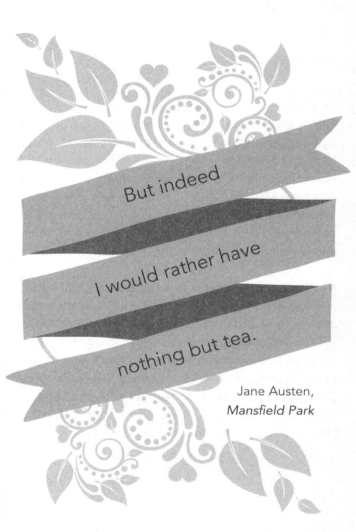

But indeed
I would rather have
nothing but tea.

Jane Austen,
Mansfield Park

Lavender tea may sound like a strange concept, and it does taste slightly of wardrobes, but it's a wonderfully refreshing and calming floral brew. Studies have shown that lavender tea can soothe indigestion and help to prevent insomnia, and it may also help with migraines. To make a cup of lavender tea, steep 1 tablespoon of dried lavender flowers in boiling water for 5 minutes, then strain and serve either plain or with a spoonful of honey.

Nettle tea is good for an immune-system boost, and the main ingredient can be found pretty much anywhere in Britain with a hint of greenery. Make sure you're wearing gloves while foraging for nettles, clipping leaves only from the top two layers of the plant. To brew, simply place 1 cup of leaves for every 2 cups of water in a pan and bring to the boil. Simmer for a few minutes and strain. Add a spot of sugar if you need to sweeten the tea a little, and enjoy.

CHAPTER 8

TEA TAKEN ON THE PAGE AND SCREEN

*Tea…
is a religion
of the art
of life.*

Okakura Kazukō

Tea drinking has had a big part to play in many works of literature and film, from eccentric tea parties to forbidden love over a pot of tea, and an awful lot of just sitting around and drinking it…

FROM THE PAGE...

Books and tea go together like Hansel and Gretel, Jekyll and Hyde or Miss Bennet and Mr Darcy. There are few corners of the literary world that have not been graced by the presence of a steaming teapot or elegant cup and saucer. From Hobbiton to Narnia, and from The Hundred Acre Wood to Pemberley, tea fuels conversation, intrigue and merriment – and many readers agree that a cup of tea is the perfect accompaniment to a lazy afternoon curled up with a book.

You can never get a cup of tea large enough or a book long enough to suit me.

C. S. Lewis

ALICE'S ADVENTURES IN WONDERLAND

Lewis Carroll's madcap Victorian children's tale features possibly the most famous tea party in the world (in the literal sense; forget Boston) – that of the Mad Hatter. Often cited as the first children's book to offer the younger generation a ticket into an imaginative fantasy world with no moral lessons to be learnt (unless you count not eating and drinking things that you find lying about), Carroll paved the way for creativity in children's books.

'Take some more tea,' the March Hare said to Alice, very earnestly.

'I've had nothing yet,' Alice replied in an offended tone: 'so I can't take more.'

'You mean you can't take less,' said the Hatter: 'it's very easy to take more than nothing.'

Lewis Carroll, *Alice's Adventures in Wonderland*

AUSTEN'S TEA

Jane Austen was clearly a fan of a good brew, with many a scene in her novels involving sitting around and the imbibing of copious amounts of tea. In fact, there's so much tea drinking in her works of fiction that there are books devoted to it (see *Tea with Jane Austen*, by Kim Wilson), while Austen aficionados claim there are some 58 references to the beverage in her six major novels (*Pride and Prejudice*, *Sense and Sensibility*, *Emma*, *Northanger Abbey*, *Persuasion* and *Mansfield Park*). Tea drinking was all the rage in Regency England, very much a social affair – and not just in the afternoon.

Sir John never came to the Dashwoods without either inviting them to dine at the Park the next day, or to drink tea with them that evening.

Sense and Sensibility

> *I should not have been at all surprised by her ladyship's asking us on Sunday to drink tea and spend the evening at Rosings. I rather expected, from my knowledge of her affability, that it would happen.*

Pride and Prejudice

And it was, it should be stressed, all about the tea…

No coffee, I thank you, for me – never take coffee. A little tea if you please.

Emma

THE IMPORTANCE OF BEING EARNEST

Oscar Wilde's Victorian farce features many a reference to tea and the ritual of taking it in the afternoon. This comedic tour de force of courtship and deception sees the two female protagonists taking a somewhat painful afternoon tea together…

Cecily: *May I offer you some tea, Miss Fairfax?*
Gwendolyn: *[With elaborate politeness.] Thank you. [Aside.] Detestable girl! But I require tea!*
Cecily: *[Sweetly.] Sugar?*
Gwendolyn: *[Superciliously.] No thank you. Sugar is not fashionable any more. [Cecily looks angrily at her, takes up the tongs and puts four lumps of sugar into the cup.]*
Cecily: *[Severely.] Cake or bread and butter?*
Gwendolyn: *[In a bored manner.] Bread and butter, please. Cake is rarely seen at the best houses nowadays.*

Cecily: [Cuts a very large slice of cake, and puts it on the tray.] Hand that to Miss Fairfax.

[Merriman and the footman serve and leave, and Gwendolyn discovers she has been insulted.]

[Gwendolyn drinks the tea and makes a grimace. Puts down the cup at once, reaches out her hand to the bread and butter, looks at it, and finds it is cake. Rises in indignation.]

Gwendolyn: You have filled my tea with lumps of sugar, and though I asked most distinctly for bread and butter, you have given me cake. I am known for the gentleness of my disposition, and the extraordinary sweetness of my nature, but I warn you, Miss Cardew, you may go too far.

Cecily: [Rising.] To save my poor, innocent trusting boy from the machinations of any other girl there are no lengths to which I would not go.

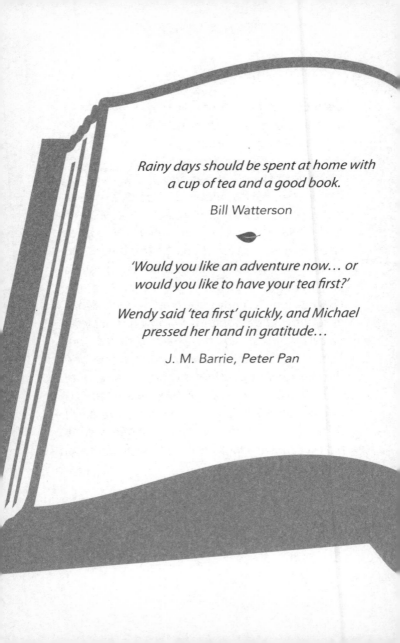

*Rainy days should be spent at home with
a cup of tea and a good book.*

Bill Watterson

*'Would you like an adventure now… or
would you like to have your tea first?'*

*Wendy said 'tea first' quickly, and Michael
pressed her hand in gratitude…*

J. M. Barrie, *Peter Pan*

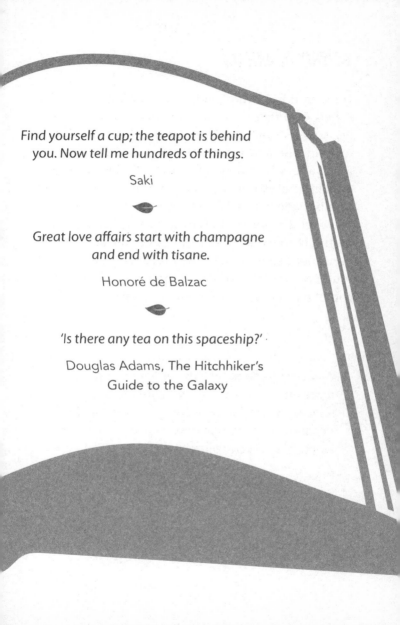

Find yourself a cup; the teapot is behind you. Now tell me hundreds of things.

Saki

Great love affairs start with champagne and end with tisane.

Honoré de Balzac

'Is there any tea on this spaceship?'

Douglas Adams, The Hitchhiker's Guide to the Galaxy

ASTERIX IN BRITAIN

Translated from the French *Asterix Chez les Bretons*, *Asterix in Britain* sees everyone's favourite Gaul and his super-strong sidekick, Obelix, head to Britain to help out as Caesar has taken the opportunity to invade while the Brits were all sitting around drinking hot water with a drop of milk. Asterix and Obelix wade in to save the day with a magic potion; however the potion goes missing and Asterix has to pretend some tea leaves in his pouch are actually the herbs needed to remake the precious stuff. The Brits triumph over the Romans under the influence of a cup of tea and declare it their national drink.

And even as he spoke, the kettle with a startling noise boiled over. This brought them to the fireside, where the easy chair was drawn cosily up, and the tea things stood ready to the sitter's elbow, the very sugar in the cup.

Robert Louis Stevenson, *Dr Jekyll and Mr Hyde*

TO THE SCREEN...

It's not only in the civilised world of literature that tea finds a home. Our favourite brew has appeared in celluloid, on screens small and large, since broadcasting began. Here are a few cinematic highlights that will have you reaching for the kettle.

MARY POPPINS

Featuring a tea party no child forgets in a hurry, 1964's Disney sensation sees Mary Poppins take tea and cake with her dependants on floating furniture just below the ceiling following an attack of laughter that causes a friend to float in mid-air. Each tea party guest must laugh their way to the ceiling in order to enjoy the suspended occasion, and sad talk causes the whole affair to sink back down to the ground.

TOY STORY

There's a nice grisly tea reference in the first of the Pixar series, with Buzz Lightyear referencing one of India's finest. Cowboy Woody discovers Lightyear at a low point, having a tea party with two headless dolls, where he laments that instead of saving the universe, he is instead taking Darjeeling with Marie Antoinette and her sister for company.

SUSPICION

Alfred Hitchcock's 1941 psychological thriller, about a wife who suspects her husband is trying to bump her off, makes a little time for tea. However, the tea scene in Suspicion has become most famous for a big continuity blooper in which Johnnie reaches for the tea and pours, and then immediately reaches for the tea and pours it again. Film pedants, eh?

GOING APE FOR A CUPPA

Some of television's most famous tea-drinkers were not people, but chimpanzees. From 1956 to the early 1980s, television advertisements for PG Tips featured chimps having tea parties, settling down for a quick break from their work digging a hole in the road with a mug of tea, or even swaggering into a saloon bar dressed as a cowboy before being served a cup of the good stuff. The most famous ad showed two chimps dressed as removal men and struggling to carry a piano down a flight of stairs.

Although times have changed, and audiences are no longer comfortable with the idea of animals dressing up and being encouraged to perform human roles – or drink tea! – the British chimps who appeared in these ads were loved and cared for by their owners, Molly Badham and Nathalie Evans, at Twycross Zoo.

The chimps' fame wasn't only restricted to teatime – one of Molly's chimps also appears in a Hammer Horror movie, T*he Revenge of Frankenstein* (1958), opposite Peter Cushing!

SCOTT PILGRIM VS. THE WORLD

The 2010 Edgar Wright film is a computer-game-themed graphic novel adaptation centred on the life and trials of Scott Pilgrim, who has to battle his girlfriend's seven evil ex-boyfriends if he wants to a) be with her and b) live. The tea reference comes when Pilgrim's girlfriend asks what kind of tea he wants. He puzzles over there being more than one type of tea; she then launches into a tongue-twister of around 20 different variants, including sleepy time, liver disaster, white truffle and vanilla walnut.

The ever-bulging tea cabinet is something I'm sure many of us can relate to in the age of the tea tsunami.

DOCTOR WHO

Not the biggest of screens, but certainly big in terms of fanbase, the earlier *Doctor Who* episodes featured a lot of tea drinking. One Doctor (John Pertwee) was so fond of tea that he allowed the tea lady into his lab, which was generally off limits; while the seventh Doctor (Sylvester McCoy) was something of a tea snob, favouring Lapsang Souchong, Earl Grey and 'Arcturan' tea, and claiming that no tea was worse than that made in a hotel room. And a more recent *Doctor Who* episode saw the eleventh Doctor (Matt Smith) revive an ill James Corden with a large amount of strong tea.

BRIEF ENCOUNTER

The love affair in 1945's *Brief Encounter* both begins and ends in the Refreshment Room at Carnforth train station in Lancashire amid many a hot cup of tea. Alec and Laura, who are both merely existing in loving yet dull marriages, strike up a friendship via the station cafe which develops into something deeper. Carnforth no longer operates as a mainline station and so has retained many of its features from the time of filming, becoming something of a pilgrimage site for mega-fans of the film. You can even sit and have a cup of Carnforth's finest in the Refreshment Room! www.refreshmentroom.com

KARATE KID, PART II

The second instalment of the 1980s classic martial arts trilogy sees Mr Miyagi and Daniel-san head to Japan for the summer. While in the land of the rising sun, Daniel takes part in a tea ceremony, performed by love interest Kumiko, all set to an oh-so romantic soundtrack – 'The Glory of Love' by Peter Cetera. Naturally, the ceremony cuts a few corners – there was a film to get on with – but viewers get the gist.

THERE IS A GREAT
DEAL OF POETRY

AND FINE SENTIMENT
IN A CHEST OF TEA.

Ralph Waldo Emerson

CHAPTER 9

TEA AND OUR HEALTH

I am so fond of tea that I could write a whole dissertation on its virtues. It comforts and enlivens without the risks attendant on spirituous liquors. Gentle herb! Let the florid grape yield to thee. Thy soft influence is a more safe inspirer of social joy.

James Boswell,
London Journal, 1762–63

Tea has been hailed for its health-giving properties from day one, when it was discovered by Chinese emperor Shennong to both revive and refresh. In Ancient China tea was not only ingested but was frequently added to creams and ointments and used as a poultice, and when it first came to Europe in the 1600s it was sold as a 'cure-all' tonic. Believed to have diuretic, stimulating and antibacterial properties, it was prescribed for everything from headaches and memory loss to stomach upsets and skin complaints.

Immortals, hear, said Jove, and cease to jar!
Tea must succeed to Wine as Peace to War.
Nor by the grape let man be set at odds,
But share in Tea, the nectar of the Gods.

Peter Motteux, 'A Poem Upon Tea'

THE SCIENCE

Although the health-promoting properties of tea were recognised by the Chinese several thousand years ago, they did also believe that it had mystical powers, but it isn't until recently that the health virtues of the *Camellia sinensis* have been decisively proven. Tea leaves contain polyphenols, which have an antioxidant effect on the body similar to some so-called 'superfoods', helping to fight off illnesses and disease, combat signs of ageing and help protect the body against cell damage. Green tea contains more polyphenols than any other tea.

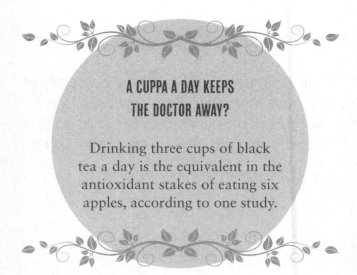

A CUPPA A DAY KEEPS THE DOCTOR AWAY?

Drinking three cups of black tea a day is the equivalent in the antioxidant stakes of eating six apples, according to one study.

If you are cold, tea
will warm you;
If you are too heated,
it will cool you;
If you are depressed,
it will cheer you;
If you are excited,
it will calm you.

William Ewart Gladstone

FIGHTING DISEASE

- Drinking green tea regularly is believed to help promote healthy blood vessels, strengthen the vascular walls of the heart and reduce the risk of coronary disease. Pu-erh (fermented) teas are thought to be particularly beneficial when it comes to lowering cholesterol as they contain naturally occurring lovastatin, which is in the present day prescribed for just that purpose – to lower cholesterol and aid weight loss.

- In its natural, uncured state, white tea has been found to have the strongest cancer-prevention properties, compared with other teas.

MENTAL STIMULATION

As well as the caffeine that many of us rely on to kick-start the day and get us moving, tea also contains the amino acid theanine, which has been found to improve both concentration and memory, as well as to help relax the mind. Theanine also works to fight the side effects of caffeine, such as headaches and raised blood pressure, so the two are perfect bedfellows.

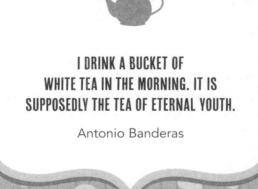

I DRINK A BUCKET OF WHITE TEA IN THE MORNING. IT IS SUPPOSEDLY THE TEA OF ETERNAL YOUTH.

Antonio Banderas

MINDFULNESS: A MEDI-TEA-TION

From the earliest times, meditation and the art of tea-making have gone hand in hand. Perhaps it's the gentle swooshing sound of water heating until it reaches a vigorous boil, perhaps it's the steam drifting through the air, or the fresh scent created when the hot water hits the leaves in the pot – whatever the reason, the sensations and rituals of tea-making have long been celebrated by the world's thinkers.

Drink your tea slowly and reverently, as if it is the axis on which the world earth revolves – slowly, evenly, without rushing toward the future.

Thích Nhất Hạnh

The Muse's friend, Tea, does our fancy aid;
Repress those vapors which the head invade;
And keeps that palace of the soul serene…

Edmund Waller, 'Of Tea'

If you ask Zen people they will say tea is not something that you pour with unawareness and drink like any other drink. It is not a drink, it is meditation; it is prayer. So they listen to the kettle creating a melody, and in that listening they become more silent, more alert.

Bhagwan Shree Rajneesh

*If you have one teapot
And can brew your tea in it
That will do quite well.
How much does he lack himself
Who must have a lot of things?*

Sen no Rikyū

*Who would then deny
that when I am sipping
tea in my tearoom I am
swallowing the whole
universe with it…?*

D. T. Suzuki

DENTAL HEALTH

In more recent years it has been discovered that tea is good for our teeth (despite staining them), helping to fight off two different types of bacteria associated with gum disease and tooth decay. Tea also contains fluoride, which is good for strengthening tooth enamel, with green tea containing twice as much fluoride as black. Green tea has also been found to neutralise bad breath, to the extent that you'll find tea extract on the list of ingredients of many toothpastes in China and Japan.

AVOID TEA AT MEALTIMES

Although tea aids digestion, it can also inhibit iron absorption and so shouldn't be consumed either half an hour before or after a meal.

It is very strange, this domination of our intellect by our digestive organs. We cannot work, we cannot think, unless our stomach wills so. It dictates to us our emotions, our passions. After eggs and bacon, it says, 'Work!' After beefsteak and porter, it says, 'Sleep!' After a cup of tea (two spoonsful for each cup, and don't let it stand more than three minutes), it says to the brain, 'Now, rise, and show your strength. Be eloquent, and deep, and tender; see, with a clear eye, into Nature and into life; spread your white wings of quivering thought, and soar, a god-like spirit, over the whirling world beneath you, up through long lanes of flaming stars to the gates of eternity!'

Jerome K. Jerome, *Three Men in a Boat*

DIY GREEN TEA FACE MASK

The antioxidants in green tea can be put to use in a number of ways, with skincare experimenters finding a green tea face mask can be just what you need to clear up an outbreak of spots, prevent blackheads or calm down reddened skin. Simply mix a spoonful of green tea leaves (alternatively you can empty a teabag) with enough clear liquid honey to form a paste and slather it all over your face. Sticky, but worth it.

FIGHT EYE BAGS WITH TEABAGS

Many dermatologists extol the virtues of used teabags as a remedy for tired eyes. The caffeine in the teabags will tighten the skin around your eyes temporarily by drawing out excess moisture, and the tannins (plant polyphenolic compounds) in tea work to reduce swelling and therefore ease the puffiness. Make sure you use black tea, though do remember to let the teabags cool down before placing them over your eyes. You'll see your morning cup of tea can wake you up in more ways than one.

Tea is the magic key to the vault where my brain is kept.

Jane Austen,
Mansfield Park

CHAPTER 10
EPILOGUE – THE FUTURE OF TEA

All true tea lovers not only like their tea strong, but like it a little stronger with each year that passes.

George Orwell

Tea drinking is steeped in thousands of years of tradition, and most people are pretty content with their own tea tastes, seeing little need to change. But with tea-drinking habits differing from country to country and the world getting smaller by the month, perhaps the future of the drink will see us embracing the practices of other cultures even more than we do already.

With the growth in popularity of Taiwanese bubble tea and health fanatics swearing a shot of green tea powder at the start of the day affords them superhuman energy, what could be next? Perhaps with the onset of climate change our summers will get hotter and we'll start to favour iced tea in that Deep South style.

It wouldn't be surprising if the herbal tea market were to continue its expansion – there being seemingly endless possibilities – and it's only a matter of time before the next super-herbal health tea is discovered. But it's interesting that the current health craze looks towards concentrated green tea – the one that started it all. What would Shennong say if he could see us twenty-first-century types knocking back our strong, lurid morning health shots? Perhaps something like: 'Why did it take you so long?'

While there

is tea,

there is hope.

Arthur Wing Pinero,
Sweet Lavender

FOREWORD BY
PIPPA GREENWOOD

FOR THE LOVE OF
RADIO 4

AN UNOFFICIAL
COMPANION

CAROLINE HODGSON

FOR THE LOVE OF RADIO 4

An Unofficial Companion

Caroline Hodgson

ISBN: 978 1 84953 642 4   £9.99   Hardback

From *Farming Today* at sunrise to the gentle strains of 'Sailing By' and the *Shipping Forecast* long after midnight, Radio 4 provides the soundtrack to life for millions of Britons. In *For the Love of Radio 4*, Caroline Hodgson celebrates all that's best about the nation's favourite spoken-word station, taking us on a tour through its history, its key personalities and programmes, and countless memorable moments from the archives.

'If you love Radio 4 it's impossible to turn it off. If you read this book it's impossible to put down.'

Charles Collingwood

'I found the book to be full of fascinating detail. It is clearly a labour of love, perfectly designed for Radio 4 lovers.'

Simon Brett

The
Birdwatcher's
Year

Richard
Williamson

THE BIRDWATCHER'S YEAR

Richard Williamson

ISBN: 978 1 84953 436 9   £9.99   Hardback

This charming and practical handbook is bursting with tips, facts and folklore to guide you through the birdwatching year. Find out how to identify birds by sight or song, everything you need to know about their behaviour, habitats and breeding and migration habits, and tips for encouraging birds into your garden. Also includes handy diary pages for making your own notes each month. A must-have for any eager birdwatcher.

'enchanting and knowledgeable'

THE SIMPLE THINGS magazine

If you're interested in finding out more about our
books, find us on Facebook at
Summersdale Publishers
and follow us on Twitter at
@Summersdale.

www.summersdale.com